THE COLLECTED POEMS
OF
PHILOMENE LONG

Copyright © 2010 Pegarty Long - Raven Productions™

Cover photo and design by Pegarty Long

Book design by DSJ Printing, Inc., Santa Monica, CA - www.dsjprinting.com

All rights reserved.

Permission to publish poems for private non-commercial use granted by The Trustees of the Philomene Long Estate.

Printed in the United States of America

First Printing: August 17, 2010

ISBN 978-1545594469

Second Printing: August 17, 2017

Published by Pegarty Long - Raven Productions™

This book available for purchase at www.raven-productions.com

THE COLLECTED POEMS
OF
PHILOMENE LONG

Edited by Pegarty Long

Introduction by John Thomas

Raven Productions Press
Venice, California USA

ACKNOWLEDGEMENTS

I would like to express deep gratitude to the following people for their help and support in publishing this book:

Mariana Dietl, Herbert B. Fishberg, Vincent Gillioz, Hammond Guthrie, Maureen Luna Long, Patrick Moore, Adam Sandman, Jim Smith and Mariano Zaro.

P.L.

Some of the poems in this book appeared in prior publications, including: The Free Venice Beachhead, *"Cold Eye Burning at 3:00 A.M."* Lummox Press; *"The Ghosts of Venice West"* Raven Productions Press; *"The Ravens"* Raven Productions Press; *"The Book of Sleep"* Momentum Press; *"Odd Phenomenon in an Abandoned City"* The Venice Temple Press; *"The Queen of Bohemia"* Lummox Press; *"The California Missions"* Kilclousha Press, Printed in the US in affiliation with the Venice Poets of America; High Performance Magazine.

1950s – The Adolescent Poems

Why Was She Smiling? 2
House of Black Gold 3
My Black Abyss 4
Insanity 5
Unspoken Prayer 6
I Walked to the Seashore 7
My Heart is Heavy With Unshed Tears 8
Which Way to Turn 9
Man in the Elevator 10
All Lies in Utter Darkness Now 11
Last Night I Wandered to the Sea 12
Then Silence 13
When Life On Earth Begins to Close 14
When Daylight Fades 15
Midnight Mass 16
Poem Written Moments After Mother's Death 17
My Sister 18

The 1960s (Early)

The Adolescent Poems 19
Poetry 20
On the Road With Pegarty 21
Fragments 25
Poet's Job 26

1970s

Nursery Rhyme 28
I Ain't the Kind that Walks on Water 29
You Don't do Much 33
Song for Roger Penney 34
I Could Tell by the Way He Smoked His Cigar 35
I Wish the Wind Would Not Blow 36
Let Me in 37
Easy Chair 38
The Visit 39

There Are No Answers	40
The Divine Violence	41
The Becoming	42
It's Not Easy to Share a Womb	43
The Unformed Beauty	44
A Painting	45
Poem for my Mother and Father	46
Fragments	47
Chalon	48
Eulogy for Stuart Z. Perkoff	49
Requiem for a Poet	50
Litany (to the Muse)	51
A Passing	52
We Waited Only for Remembrance	53
Prayer	54
She	55

1980s (Early to Middle)

An Ancient Race of Queens	62
I Am the Poem	63
Odd Phenomenen in An Abandoned City	64
Pastorale	66
Venice (on the Poetry Wall in Venice, California)	68
Venice (Original)	69
John Thomas	70
Twenty Years	71
Death on the Santa Monica Freeway	72
Cold Eye at 3 a.m.	74
Three Haiku	75
Eyes of a Ghost	76
The Hour of the World	77
You and I Now Living	78
Nightly Vigils	79
The Circle	80
Rooms Without Walls	81
The Closing	82

The Cats	83
A Shadow	84
The Moon	85
Your Kiss (Was It a Kiss?)	86
I Remember	87
Three Love Poems from the Japanese	88
Love, You are Green and Dark	89
Wedding Poem	90
Summer '85, Venice	91
This is the Morning	92
John Thomas	95
Handle This, Big Guy	96
Seduction Poem	97
You are Sleeping, My Love	98
John Thomas, Stretched Upon the Bed	99
A Love Poem / A Death Poem	100
I Am Reminded it is Spring	102
Reason is Cruel	103
I Am No Longer Afraid	104
The Poem Takes a Hundred Years to Come	105
Every Poem I Write	106
The Hermit	107
My Maxims	108
Letters to Pope John Paul II	110
Poem for my Mother	116

The Cold Ellison Poems (1987-1989)

Cold Ellison I	118
Cold Ellison II	121
Cold Ellison III	123
Cold Ellison IV	125
Cold Ellison V	127
Cold Ellison VI	129
Cold Ellison VII	131

The California Mission Poems

Introduction *134*
Junipero Serra *135*
La Purisima *136*
San Juan Bautista.. *137*
San Fernando Mission *138*
Carmel.. *139*
Mission San Diego de Alcala *140*
Mission San Antonio de Padua................................... *141*
Soledad *142*
San Miguel Mission *143*
Mission San Luis Rey *145*
San Juan Capistrano... *146*

Mass for the Dead

Introit *148*
Gradual.. *149*
Epistle *150*
Gospel *151*
Communion *152*
Post Communion *153*

Ireland Poems

Ireland *156*
Stone Circle of Drombeg *157*
Grass, Stone, Wind.. *159*
The Tall Towers of Ireland *161*

Late 1980s

The Flowers: Are They Truly Evil? *164*
Thats It! John and I Are Packed *165*
Old Fool!.. *166*
Atrial Fibrillation *167*
Whispers.. *168*
I, Too, Died.. *169*
Wedding Poem for Rachel and Mark *170*
Immense Red Rose of Beijing *171*

He Was Choking Me.. *172*
Why I Do Not Read the L.A. Times *173*
Plant III.. *174*
San Francisco Earthquake...*175*
The Moth... *176*
There is No Comfort.. *177*

1990s

Venice Woman Tossing Terra Cotta Planter, Hits Gunman ... *180*
A Voice for Those Who Have No Voice................................... *182*
Cemetery in the Sand *183*
Palaces and Colonnades *185*
Memoirs of a Nun on Fire.. *186*
L.A. Riot Poem *191*
Los Angeles Earthquake *195*
Cold Ellison VIII... *197*
Great Zen Funeral... *198*
Observations on the Color Black.. *202*
Portrait of my Daughter.. *203*
Sonnet for John Thomas..*204*
Poem for my Daughter.. *205*
Black Buddha in a Dark Alley *206*
Hermits in Greater Los Angeles *207*
An Ordinary Day of Writing *208*
My Sister the Painter *209*
America: On the Rails *210*
Oh! Allen, Howl For Us With Your Ghostly Tongue.............. *214*
Jack Micheline Through the Eyes of a Dying Cockroach.......... *215*
Eulogy for William Margolis *217*
Eulogy for Shirley Clarke *219*
In Pegarty's Burgundy Room *220*
Roger Penney, Death Cannot Close your Eyes........................ *221*
The Paintings, Somehow, Must Have Felt It *223*
Poems are the World Asleep...*224*
Dropped Under the Skin of Life.. *225*
Poem for my Father *226*

Crushed Pigeon with the Secret *227*

A Monstrous Root *229*

The Hunger *230*

Marriage Vows *231*

I Write as the Muse Requires *232*

Mirrors are Sleeping Winds *233*

The Poem a Scalpel *234*

Last Confession *235*

The Ghosts of Venice West *237*

Poem To An Unborn *238*

The Raven Poems

Nine Ways of Looking at a Raven *240*

Cry of the Ravens *241*

There are Never Enough Ravens in a Poem *243*

A book of hours

The Annunciation *246*

Nativity *247*

The Crucifixion *248*

Easter *249*

Pentecost *250*

2000s

Poem for my Son *252*

Pink Cloud Poem *254*

Wedding Poem *255*

Romance Among the Morning Glories (High but Subtle) *256*

Questions *257*

Adam *258*

Aidan *259*

Maureen *260*

In the Privacy of Mirrors *261*

Pegarty Pegarty Pegarty *262*

The Pacific *263*

The Sea *264*

Fragments *265*

Poem to Lost Poems *266*
I Am Not of This World *267*

2002

Cold Ellison IX *270*
19th Anniversary Poem *271*
Pieta at Holy Cross Cemetery *274*
Pieta in a Los Angeles Mortuary *275*
At the Cemetery, June 2002 .... *276*
She's a Ms. Prufrock *277*
The Poem Transfers Its Force to the Reader *278*
John and I: Our Own Country Now, Eternal Present *279*
Because Death, You Are So Successful *280*
Marcus Aurelius at a Dodger Game; Kirk Gibson up to Bat *281*
Ingredients of Grief *285*
Found Poem *286*
A Swan in the Cemetery's Pond *287*
Where Else Do Walls Glow Like this? *288*
Inside This Bleeding Lyric *289*

Prose 2002-2006

How to Get Along with your Mother, Father, Sister, Brother, Every Last One of your Children, your Grandmother, Grandfather, Grandson and Granddaughter *292*
Socrates at the White House *294*
Aristotle at a Laker Game and the Poetics of Kobe Bryant *298*
Inauguration Poem for Bill Rosendahl *301*
Poet Laureate Acceptance Speech *303*

Final Poems

Poetry is the Door to Infinity *306*
Bug Poem for a Three-Year-Old *307*
Scripture of the Muse *308*
This Room; This Burning City *309*
I Dream in 2,200 Different Languages *310*
Far Away Now *311*
Whispers Before a Tomb (of my Husband, Poet John Thomas) *313*

Three Haiku	*315*
America	*316*
Is there a Reciprocity?	*317*
Litany for Pegarty	*318*
One Dies Happily	*319*
Cold Ellison IX	*320*
I Wish to Die in the Last Thrust of	*323*

Photographs

Plates I through XXVIII follow page 323

PREFACE
by Pegarty Long

This first edition of the collected poems of *Philomene Long*, published on August 17th, 2010 which would be her 70th birthday, is an autobiographical journey of the poet's poetic inner life. It chronicles the internal journey and the growth of the poem within the poet from the years of her adolescence to the year of her death in 2007.

"These are poems about the act of writing a poem – to see at close quarters how poems are made – so deep it is almost impossible to speak about – the act at times euphoric, at times terrifying." - Philomene Long.

The poems are set in the order that she intended. The writing and style has been kept intact with only minor changes made when found necessary. Photographs are included to represent the history, and some of the people and the places (both here and gone) that took some part in this most magnificent life.

Introduction
by John Thomas

Philomene Long has always had a preference for the extreme. She has preferred the company of a St. Francis of Assisi, taking his clothes off in public, or a Joan of Arc, who heard voices and dressed in men's clothing, has preferred to live among the poets, saints and mad ones of Venice West, with those who live a life of dedicated poverty.

Because Philomene has believed in the Beatitudes, *"Blessed are the poor in spirit"* (or *"emptiness"* in Zen terms), she has power. She has: once stood in the center of a room on fire without one strand of hair being singed; once accidentally drank twice the lethal dose of a deadly poison and lived; has raised up this three hundred pound author and thrown him across a bed; has limbered her way out of his impossible-to-break wrestler's cradle hold; has chased a rapist off Venice Beach, his engorged penis still in his hand. During the great Los Angeles earthquake of 1994, she stood upright (in order to feel the force of it through the souls of her feet) and her feet glowed. At this moment, as I write, she glows.

Her mother had come to New York from Ireland, as a young woman, to be a writer. Philomene was born in Greenwich Village, which in those days was full of poets and saints of Art, writing and painting, carousing and leaping out of windows. At age fifteen she was infused by the Muse of poetry and began writing. (Her mother would allow her to stay home from school when Philomene told her she had a poem in her.) At eighteen she became a nun, cloistered in a convent atop a mountain high above Los Angeles. After five years of living in an enclosure of silence she escaped down the side of a mountain in the middle of the night into the world of angel headed hipsters and Zen saints of Venice West where she became the Queen of Bohemia.

She, mind you, still follows her vocation, still considers herself a nun. She was Stuart Perkoff's muse figure and love at the end of his life. She studied Zen for twenty-one years with Taizan Maezumi Roshi, until his death in 1985, and for nearly two decades she has studied patience and tolerance, employing me as her practice subject. Now, she is also a kind of Zen priestess.

How does Philomene live? Which means, since we're together, how do we live? The life of art (Art?), the life of dedicated poverty. She says it well: that our love is the religion, the only religion and that no matter how wrongheaded we become it will always bring us back to it.

Philomene is a poet. A great poet. I envy her genius. Her genius on the page: the words get in the way.

What else should I tell you of Philomene? Something she doesn't like my speaking of, so perhaps I'll sneak this passage in without showing it to her: Philomene is a woman of amazing and seemingly imperishable beauty. And she is my Muse.

Poetry is my passion – as is, of course, my muse and lady, Philomene. Yeats said somewhere (speaking of writing), that he hoped to 'go empty to the grave.' Not I. My wish would be to fall dead on my face, pen on paper, or in Philomene's embrace. Or, (admittedly difficult to arrange) both at once. Hand over blank paper—in the embrace of Philomene—if possible (difficult to manage) both at once.

1950s

The Adolescent Poems

WHY WAS SHE SMILING?

Her name is Sally Benedict. She is young and beautiful and dead. Yeh, she's dead alright. They told me for sure. Don't look very dead though. It's too bad it had to happen. I liked Sally, do now anyway. Always so pretty. Always the smiles. Liked her dog, Mister Smitty. Good dog... manner... A wag of the tail for me, anyway, when I came by. She was mad at Mister Smitty that day, the day she died. Grew up together is what we did. A good time we had of it too. Always together we were. Always the comparing. No manners. People have no manners.

I won't like it – the being dead part. Full of fun she was. Always the kidding, always the joke on me. "I fooled you, I fooled you," she'd giggle. Always one step ahead of me, she was. But I didn't mind... only sometimes. I bet I get her clothes.

I'm remembering that time in the flower field. We swung and swung around to see who would get the dizziest the fastest. Her face began to do all sorts of things. Looked like a angel one turn, a monster the next. Guess she was too busy laughing to notice my face. Or mine was funny or something. Kinda hard to think of her so still now. I mean, she was always dancing around or had some trick up her sleeve for you. But I tricked her this time.

Sally sure looks pretty lying there, so natur'l. Almost like she's smiling. Pretty white dress too. Looks just like she's smiling. She fell out of her window is what she did. She was in that room of hers just singin' and dancin'. She got mad at Mister Smitty and hit him. But that didn't stop her. She went right on having a good time. Mister Smitty just walked right over to me to show me how he felt. He felt the same as I do. She kept on dancing. It is too bad it had to happen.

The men are coming to take her away. Goodbye Sally. You were the loveliest thing I ever knew. It's like I'm going down there with you. They're covering you up now. You won't tell them will you, Sally? She's gone for good now, I know she is. She sure looked like she was smiling there. Almost like a real smile, the one she gave you when she had a trick for you. I wonder why she was smiling. Those men are staring at me. They are staring at me. Why was she smiling?

— Fall, 1955 (Age 15)

HOUSE OF BLACK GOLD

While passing through Bristol
I once heard told
Of the strange things that happen
In the House of Black Gold
The forbidden House of Black Gold.

There's said that a maiden
With hair like the sun
Once lived in the house
And here met her doom
Here, in the House of Black Gold.

She is said to have nursed
Her love's soul from the dead
And because of this deed
Was condemned to behead.
This in the House of Black Gold.

Condemned as a witch
 She was sent to the stake
And went to her death
With an unending laugh
This in the House of Black Gold.

Now they say when dusk fades
To the black sheet of night
You can still hear her laughing
Beneath the moon's light.
All this in the House of Black Gold.

She searches the halls
For her head and her hair
And the soul of her love
Which is said to be there.
There, in the House of Black Gold.

So when in Bristol remember
The story of old
And be sure to stay clear
Of the House of Black Gold
The forbidden House of Black Gold.

—*1955 (Age 15)*

MY BLACK ABYSS

Here I stand –
Two steps from death
Beneath me, a black abyss
It calls.
And breathes it's wanting kiss.
It calls.

My first step taken
I stop, I ponder
No hope, no love, alone
Nothing.
My body moves...
It lies there crumbled in the
Bottomless
My soul, in the bottomless
Black abyss
Nothing.

— 1955 (Age 15)

INSANITY

Moments pass by in emptiness.
Confined by the curtain of life before.
Unbent with time's gentle whisper.
Unceasing with destiny's roar.

Apart from the world left behind me.
Where terror and sorrow doth trod.
A darkness obscure from all light.
And only one hope – my God.

—1955 (Age 15)

UNSPOKEN PRAYER

A faint suggestion of a smile
Upon her lips.
And yet a tear falls
From her saddened eyes.
She stands aimlessly for a while,
then turns,
and leaves.
A grayness fills the skies.

She walks alone through the empty dark
In thought.
And feels the softness
Of the moistened air.
God had called the one she loved so dear.
Leaving a lasting mark.
She and her love alone would share
A secret so great as an
Unspoken prayer.

—1955 (Age 15)

I WALKED TO THE SEASHORE

I walked to the seashore,
And gazed at the sea.
My heart light with hope,
As I ran breathlessly.

The wind hit my face,
And I laughed at my cares.
The stars seemed to sing,
The moon smiled and stared.

I fell to the ground,
And the sand seemed to say,
"Your prayers will be answered."
"Your hope will stay."

I picked up the stick,
Tossed it into the sea.
And a wave like a tyrant,
Brought it back to me.

I thought of my hope,
As the stick I just threw,
Coming back with its beauty,
With love all anew

The next time I threw it
My love was my thought,
Returning much faster,
With kindness I sought.

With my hope and my love,
Again it was tossed.
The waves beat with violence,
And the stick – it was lost.

—1955 (Age 15)

MY HEART IS HEAVY WITH UNSHED TEARS

My heart is heavy with unshed tears
Burdened with unescapable fears.

(My God! Help me!
I have no one but Thee)

I sought love in friends,
with no relief.
In another's sorrow,
and found, but grief.

No quench for yearning thirst,
no love, secure.
No happiness. But pain,
to long endure.

(My God! Love me!
I have no one but Thee)

—1955 (Age 15)

WHICH WAY TO TURN

Which way to turn.
Which way to go.
Without God's help.
I'd never know.

When troubles never
Seem to cease.
God guides me to
My inner peace.

There is no need
For my despair.
For when I ask
He's always there.

—1955 (Age 15)

MAN IN THE ELEVATOR

(This is the first poem that was not only work for me, but I realized that the poem was not working. Mother had allowed me to stay home from school because I told her I had this poem in me. I recall thinking, while I agonized over it: "This is work!" It was more difficult than going to school.)

Long ago, when I was young,
And everything was gay
With carefree child's adventures
And wonders of each day

I, by chance, once road inside
A crowded elevator.
Though only moments seemed to pass.
I would remember later —-

A tired old man close my me,
With understanding eyes.
Who wore a look of loneliness,
And yet a smile so wise.

His aged lines upon his face,
Showed kindness in his life.
With love, truth, and sorrow,
And pain's of living's strife.

The elevator came to stop.
He moved slowly to the door.
My heart some how grew heavy
Knowing I'd see him no more.

He turned around before he left
And looking straight at me.
Silently, he whispered,
"My dear, please pray for me."

My childhood years have passed.
With thoughts of fun and laughter.
Returning at times with cheery smiles
Of then and life hereafter.

But each night when I kneel down to pray
The thought still comes to me.
"God bless the man in the elevator,
Wherever he may be."

— 1955 (Age 15)

ALL LIES IN UTTER DARKNESS NOW

All lies in utter darkness now.
A tiny snowflake flitters down.
Beneath the dancing shadows lie,
Two bodies in the ground.

The sun is like a tyrant,
It's rays shown as a guide.
Beneath the dancing shadows,
The dead lay side by side.

For once the two had loved,
Locked in the bounds of sin.
Apart from light and truth,
Where darkness does begin.

Now they are together
Escaped from goodness' glow.
In pain, cold, and darkness.
Eternity below.

— 1955 (Age 15)

LAST NIGHT I WANDERED TO THE SEA

Last night I wandered to the sea
Until it turned eleven
T'was the sweetest night I ever saw
As though a taste of heaven.

The place had all the charms
It used to have before
Yet had you been right there with me
I would have liked it more.

But that not being and I alone
It was no more to me
Than just another sandy shore
And just another sea.

— 1955 (Age 15)

THEN SILENCE

He lay with his eyes closed, and slowly began to drift into silent nothingness. He reached for something being, yet it had none. Although unheard, his self cried out. His soul wandered from his body until they were no longer one... then silence.

— 1955 (Age 15)

WHEN LIFE ON EARTH BEGINS TO CLOSE

(Herein rhythmic influence of Emily Dickinson.)

When life on earth
Begins to close,
And only death awaits.
Will I be in the
Hands of God,
To meet my inevitable fate?

Will I cast the vandal
From my soul
Away to hell's torment?
And ban the sickness
From within.
Will my poor heart lament?

When my bed of death
Is empty
And the candle light grows dim.
Will I leave my bed
To spend
Eternity with Him?

— 1955

WHEN DAYLIGHT FADES

(With this poem I learned the meaning of "cliche." When showing this poem to my mother she advised me that the word "fades" in this context was a cliche. I had thought I had been observant and was proud of coming up with the word. I was happy for her advise and later I saw that the poem was little more than cliche.)

When daylight fades
To evening dusk
And stars awake to breathe
Their heavenly light
My heart shows forth
It's fondest cares
My two loves

When the earth is still,
And all sleep
Beneath the silent coat
Of darkest night
My soul turns to
Its resting place.
My two loves.

— 1955 (Age 15)

MIDNIGHT MASS

It's Midnight Mass.
The church is still.
All hearts are light.
Filled with good will.

The choir sings.
The people pray.
And all await
The coming day.

The Child of God
Is born again.
This time it's in
The hearts of men.

— 1955 (Age 15)

POEM WRITTEN MOMENTS AFTER MOTHER'S DEATH

Heaven kissed her
Smiled
And wanted her.

Heaven took her –
Gently –
And loved her.

—March 31, 1958 (Age 17)

MY SISTER

(Only poem saved from convent, although so many written.)

Among grass and trees she walked.
Small flowers touch her feet. Her
beauty gathered nature in one face—
And nature smiled.

— Summer 1959

The 1960s
(Early)

POETRY

(Lines written on envelope the day before escape from convent.)

Poetry –
the door to infinity

— 1963 (Age 23)

ON THE ROAD WITH PEGARTY AND HOW I RELINQUISHED MY VIRGINITY IN THE RAIN IN A GUTTER IN ENGLAND WITH A SAILOR OFF THE "QUEEN MARY"
(and what followed that)

EXCERPTS

This is a sexual memoir. This is not a sexual memoir. It tells of the years after I escaped from the convent in the middle of the night into the world of poetry and Zen. I am writing for my daughter who recently asked how was it that I, a Catholic nun, seemingly remained a nun in the world and not have sexual guilt.

The Atlantic. 1963.

After five years cloistered in a Catholic convent above Los Angeles, I escaped down the side of a mountain in the middle of the night, went on the road and with my sister Pegarty, across America, then hopped on the "Queen Mary" and was sailing the Atlantic towards Europe. The first night on the great ship was like a night in the cloister: dark and silent. There was an electrical problem and the stabilizer had failed. The ship rolled in absolute darkness until it leaned almost parallel to the ocean. I surmised this because all I could see was ocean when I looked out the porthole.

Then would begin the great list of the ship to the opposite side. As the ship rolled there was little sense of time, but I would guess that with each tilt from one side and back to the upright position took about an hour. Then it would all begin again.

I was not so much afraid as interested. It was all too big for fear. While I was slowly rolling inside the great, dark, belly of the "Queen Mary" I had my first thought to have sex.

I still feel this was a grand time and place to have this idea.

The most important travel tip I have ever been given was from the nuns. It was "Never go anywhere without a book." (This was meant for traveling even a few feet out the door.) I took this seriously because those nuns were usually right. But it was too dark to read a book so I had that thought instead.

So the next day, while standing upon the long wooden boards of the starboard deck, I decided with whom this would take place. It would be with a sailor off of the "Queen Mary." His name was Barry Thomas. I chose him because he read books and had bright blue oceanic eyes. I didn't tell him what I had in mind but we agreed to meet shortly after the ship docked in South Hampton.

That night inside the slowly rocking womb-like belly of the "Queen Mary" I had concluded that sex was not sin.

England. South Hampton.

The next day in the cold, damp South Hampton night I, dressed like a sailor myself in a light blue middy blouse and white pleated skirt, met Barry, sailor of the "Queen Mary" at an appointed spot where I leaned against a tree and said: "I want you to be the first." He said he was very moved that I had chosen him to be the first and that he had been imagining me naked every time he saw me on the deck of the ship. And then it began to rain – soft, soft English rain.

And we moved to a dark alley for privacy—and the rain still failing gently beginning to soak my blue and white sailor outfit as we lay down in a gutter and Barry entered me as the rain poured more forcefully until it was as though we were underwater and it felt just like that –it felt like being the ocean — all the pouring and rolling in the dark with only a dim streetlight (like a light house in the distance), rain flowing over my face and through my hair, my virginal blood mingling with rain flowing down the gutter drain. It seemed, to me, sacramental so I thought of one of the first sentences they have God saying in the Old Testament in Genesis— "And God saw that all he made was very good."

And I know it was good for Barry too because he kept singing "When my life is through and the angels ask me to recall the thrill of it all, I'll tell them I remember, I'll tell them I remember, I'll tell them I remember you."*

He said that everyone remembers the first time and that I would remember him. And he was right. I do remember him. Barry Thomas of Hull, England.

Travel plans.

As the 'Queen Mary" was pulling into the harbor of South Hampton Pegarty had gone over our finances. She told me that we had $260.00 each to last for 6 months. While standing on the deck overlooking England approaching, we recalled how people had commented on our courage to travel Europe without being a part of a tour or have any hotel reservations. It seemed that no one was doing that kind of thing in those days – especially two women. At the precise moment the great ship stopped I said: "Maybe it is not courage but stupidity."

Our travel plan would be to cross the continent, knapsacks on backs, sleeping in an occasional bed and breakfast or hostel but mostly on trains, and thumbing rides across Europe. And the travel plan began immediately. With no hotel reservations (after my 'When my life is through and the angels ask me to recall the thrill of it all" experience), Pegarty and I spent our first night in England sleeping – while standing up in one of those beautiful bright red English telephone booths.

Performed by Frank Ifield. Written by Victor Schertzinger and Johnny Mercer 1962

Germany. Berlin.

This is about how I lowered two unwanted erections while in Berlin.

I take full responsibility for what happened in Germany.

My first mistake was to shout in a Berlin bar: "I CAN DRINK ANYONE HERE UNDER THE TABLE!" I take full responsibility for what followed.

The bartender placed two small drinks before me, one iridescent blue, the other iridescent green. He whispered: "Anyone who drinks these two together blacks out."

I drank the blue. I drank the green. And as a chaser— a large glass of cherry red wine. I did not black out and I did drink everyone under the table. Only two silhouettes of men were left standing.

But then, they had not been drinking.

"Need a place to stay tonight?"

I did need a place to stay. I suppose my fellow-traveling sister Pegarty and I, with knapsacks at our knees, had the no-place-to-stay look on our faces. We were accustomed to having that expression because of our habit of arriving in a town late at night with no place to stay and no money changed into local currency.

The two men brought us to a gritty apartment. Pegarty stumbled over the threshold. She hadn't made the challenge I had made, but had gone along in some fashion. I guided her to the back room and gently lay her down to sleep on a grimy bed, then returned to the living room where the two Germans were waiting for me on the couch with rampant erections. I sat on another couch, facing them. Thinking of my sister passed out in the back room, so vulnerable, I decided on a course which turned out to be the appropriate choice.

I began to bore them. (To bore them *purposely*. There is a difference.) I spoke in a monotone with unending sentences, no periods or commas, and repeated myself over and over and over. It was their faces that began to soften first, with the pain of listening — just small points of pain initially, then their whole faces.

Then they began to deflate simultaneously. I could feel the erections sagging without actually seeing them, especially when there were two at the same time. Even after they were down I talk and talk and talk to make sure that there was no possibility of their return. I cannot let this happen because my sister is in her wine dark sleep in the back room.

I sat erect as the nuns had taught me.

I used long vowels, as in "slow" and " low" and inserted them into long sentences, over and over. It is so boring that I was about to topple myself but, with Emily Dickinson, I continued to sit erect.

While talking I remembered one of the basic laws of physics — that for every action there is an equal reaction, and I began to understand that it applies to words as well. It was happening right there, right then. My boring action was having an equally boring reaction. I was arranging molecules with my tongue. I was discovering the physics of linguistics. The men, with their depleted erections, are in pain — pain inflicted upon them by the long vowel. Its lulling force propelled them out of the room. I saw the backs of their heads as they went out the door and I collapsed on the dirty couch. That's how close I came to wordless extinction.

I blacked out on that couch. My bodily functions also collapsed for when I awoke in the morning I realized that I had urinated in my sleep through my thick black woolen skirt, at the same time remembering I had arranged to meet a lovely German gentleman for breakfast.

While I ran across Berlin to meet my German gentleman, it began to rain. It ran down my grimy face and soaked my thick black skirt and black sweater. I could not see that my face was turning into mud but realized that it must be when I saw the falling rain cover the backs of my hands with sludge.

I don't know how Pegarty got to the gentleman's flat—just that she had been awakened by the real owner of the apartment coming home and screaming at her for being in his bed. But finally we were with Peter, who had brought along a man named Klaus. And as a breakfast treat he had also brought (how could he have known of my night of red wine green and blue drinks, or of my green, blue and red hangover?) a bottle of red wine and a box of chocolates.

Peter, with great gentility, poured a glass and offered a chocolate, which I ate along with the wine, and was more aware than I would have liked to have been the last evening's ghastly red, green and blue alcoholic rainbow mixing in my gaseous abdomen..

He then reached over the table and took my right hand — the hand (by this time the rain had created little streams running through the mud) looking as if it belonged to the Creature from the Black Lagoon. No. Worse. It was the hand of the Creature rising out of a sewer.

He kissed it, saying, "You ... "

(Here, a long pause.)

"Have ... " (Another long pause)

"You have the hand ... " (Pause) " ... of a.... "

(Here an enormously long pause)

" ... a, a, a woman."

"You have the hand of a WOMAN!"

That is the end of this story. And it is a fine ending.

FRAGMENTS

The velvet claw
Of a mother-in-law.

— 1965

An orange is
So loud

— 1967

After death of Baby Cahiermie –
Out of the loss of purpose – intensity.

— March 6, 1967

POET'S JOB

Poet's job –
To get what is dormant in us to the surface.
I guess what I mean to say is "Thou art God."

— August 17, 1967

1970s

NURSERY RHYME

For my daughter.

I had a mother
Whose name was Maureen,
Who dressed me in white
And taught me to sing
Songs of fairies
That lay over my head
And she read to me stories of Queens.

I have a daughter
Whom I call Maureen,
Who likes to wear white
And to sing
And be Queen
And she tells me of things
In the sky that she's seen.

—1971

I AIN'T THE KIND THAT WALKS ON WATER

(Song)

You're packing to go
Taking the train at nine
Saying, you're tired of my fussin'
Fixing live life real fine
Well, are you tired of my kissin'
With my big, big red lips
Are you tired of my dancin'
With my fine dancing hips

Well, I ain't the kind
That walks on water
But I say you're going to be lonely
For a long, long time
No, I ain't the kind that walks on water
But I say you're going to be lonely
For a long, long, time

You'll get on that train
And smile as the whistle blows
Well, it doesn't hurt now, honey
But wait, it's gonna show
When you wake up next morning
And there's no sweet smelling me
You'll be crying in that bed, honey
You'll be crying desperately
You'll be crying on that train home again
You'll be crying at my front door
But I won't be here, honey
I won't be here anymore

(refrain)

'Cause I ain't the kind that walks on water
But I say you're going to be lonely
For a long, long time
No, I ain't the kind that walks on water
But I say you're going to be lonely
For along, long time

So put back those undershirts
And that nice sweater I gave you
I don't want you to be lonely
For a long, long time
Do you think something's the matter with me?
I just don't want you to be lonely for a long, long time

(AD LIB)

You just set yourself right down here...
No, I don't want you to be lonely for a long time
Yes. Put back that undershirt...

(refrain)

'Cause I ain't the kind that walks on water
But I say you're going to be lonely
For a long, long time
No, I ain't the kind that walks on water
But I say you're going to be lonely
For a long, long time

I Ain't The Kind That Walks on Water

Music & Lyrics Philomene Long

You're packing to go - Taking the train at nine saying, you're tired of my fussin' fixing live life real fine. Well, are you tired of my kissin' with my big big red lips Are you tired of my dancin' with my fine dancing hips? Well, I ain't the kind __ That walks on water but I say you're going to be lonely for a long long, time. No, I ain't the kind __ That walks on water but I say you're going to be lonely for a long long, time. You'll get on that train And smile as the whistle blows. Well, it doesn't hurt now, honey but wait, it's gonna show. When you wake up next morning and there's no sweet smelling me you'll be

I Ain't The Kind That Walks on Water

2

12 cry - ing in that bed, ho - ney you'll be cry - ing des - pe-rate-ly. You'll be

13 cry - ing on that train home a - gain you'll be cry - ing at my front door. But I

14 won't be here, ho-ney I won't be here a-ny-more 'Cause I ain't the kind that walks on wa - ter but I

16 say you're going to be lone-ly for a long long, time. No, I ain't the kind That walks on wa - ter but I

18 say you're going to be lone - ly for a long long, time

19 Spoken Words ad lib

So put back those undershirts
And that nice sweater I gave you   'Cause
I don't want you to be lonely
For a long, long time
Do you think something's the matter with me?
I just don't want you to be lonely for a long, long time

20 I ain't the kind that walks on wa - ter but I say you're going to be lone-ly for a long long, time. No,

22 I ain't the kind that walks on wa - ter but I say you're going to be lone-ly for a long long, time.

YOU DON'T DO MUCH

(For John Thomas before we came together.)

(Song)

You don't do much
But what you do is good
You don't say much
But what you say you should
I like being
A fine friend of yours
Cause, Honey,
It relaxes me

You've got strong arms
And a strong head too
You do the kind of things
That stroooong people do
You're soft in the middle
And I like that too
Cause, Honey,
It relaxes me

You're not always right
And you're not always wrong
You don't have a home
But you seem to belong
There's something about you
That makes me sing songs
Cause, Honey,
It relaxes me

SONG FOR ROGER PENNEY

(Song)

You have filled me with your seas
Your moons all move in me
Your birds fly
Through the wide skies
That are now my eyes

I have given you my mountains
My trees at rest
My seed blooms
In the soft winds
That are now your breath

Our rivers never sleep
Our stars extend
Wide within our love
Where there is no end.

I COULD TELL BY THE WAY HE SMOKED HIS CIGAR

(Song)

He said he liked fine women
And that I was fine and true
He said he liked them handsome
And that I would do
But I could tell by the way he smoked his cigar
That that man would never sing the blues
I could tell by the way he smoked his cigar, Ma
That man would never sing the blues.

And then I heard him laughing
Underneath my windowsill
And then I saw him dancing
Down the road to Lucille's
And then I heard THEM laughing\AS they left
in her brand new limousine car
And there I was standing again
Beneath my bad luck star.
But I could tell by the way he smoked his cigar
That man would never sing the blues,
I could tell by the way he smoked that cigar, Ma
That man would never sing the blues.

And now I have a daughter
And I live on wine and booze
But I can tell by the way she chews her gum'
That she'll never sing the blues
I can tell by the way she chews her gum, Ma
That girl will never sing the blues.

—1974

I WISH THE WIND WOULD NOT BLOW

(From the "Egocentric Blues Series.)

(Song)

I wish the wind would not blow
I wish that time would go
When you came tonight to me
When you, dear, came tonight.

I wish the flowers could not grow
I wish the sun could not flow
When you came tonight to me
When you, dear, came tonight

But time went on as before
Because joy is hard to leave but it's not our own
When you went tonight from me
When you, dear, went tonight.

LET ME IN

(For Stuart Z. Perkoff)
From the "Egocentric Blues Series.)

(Song)

Lord, I asked you
If you would please let me in
But you didn't take me
You just took my friend

You know it gets lonely down here, Lord
And it gets hard to hold your head real high
I just want to see your pretty face
I want to rest in you shiny sky

So could you please send one of your angels
To come help me to fly
I won't bother anyone
I'll be real quiet

Because, Lord, you know I asked you
If I could please, please come in
But I think you didn't hear me, Lord
'Cause you just took my friend.

EASY CHAIR

(From the "Egocentric Blues Series.)

(Song)

I've seen too much of what
I've been fall down
(Come sit in my easy chair
I'll fix you some lemonade)

And I've had too many
Holy words do me wrong
(I know it's hot outside
But it's cool here in the shade)

I don't know what I've lost
Or what I've found
But it's nice here with you
And this song has an easy
Kind of sound.

THE VISIT

I never thought it would be like this. I thought
I would be in white. I thought
I would smell like flowers when you spoke. Yes. I am
Alone. Yes. I've let things go. I was not
Expecting you so late. I thought it would be day
And my house clean. I thought I would be young.
I thought things would be different.

My flowers have grown up and died.
I have left them here for you. I think
They're pretty this way too. Brown and gold
And they stay in one position. Not like other
Flowers do. When you're alone flowers
Can make you nervous. They move about.
They get so fast when things
Get slow.

But I am glad you came. And that we could have
This talk. Now I no longer have to wait.
am sorry you have to go.
It was so slow before you came. It will be
Much slower after you go. I think
It will stop.

THERE ARE NO ANSWERS

There are no answers
There are a few poems

THE DIVINE VIOLENCE

We await
The strike
Of the Divine Violence
The incision to be made
For the penetration of fire
The opening
The shrill of the impaled
Pinned to the Holy Waters
Of the Alluring One
A new beauty born
Thrashes to shed its shell
If God could God would weep
With the torn, the ruptured
Ecstasies

THE BECOMING

It is not the end
But the becoming
It is not the beginning
But the becoming
It is the becoming
The becoming
The becoming
The seed sprays the scent
The scent the mystery
The mystery the unraveling
The unraveling
The unraveling
The dissolve
The cut
The pruning
The opening flesh flower
Seed inside seed
Womb within womb
Becoming
Becoming
Becoming
The joy is becoming
The joy is becoming
It is coming
It is coming
The becoming is joy
The becoming is joy
The seed
The scent
The spray
The mystery
Raveling
Unraveling
In the joy
Of the becoming

IT'S NOT EASY TO SHARE A WOMB

It's not easy to share a womb
It is two soggy toads scratching at each other
waking you up from your soggy eyed womb dreams.
There is no room.
No flap the wing
No room to spread the sparsely formed breast
to flap the wing
to kick the web
to scratch for your blood hungry organs
to feed your thirst for womb blood.

It is not easy to be the deep unborn
while the world expands in spinning white
and you, the four armed four legged
push for the light
tug at the inflexible womb skin
as that scratched calloused membrane holds its host
close in the unwanted warmth.

Once there was ease
Before the watery eye could see
Sightless, before the implantation took root to bloom
within the blurry blue veined walls.
There were no twins in those celestial winds.

THE UNFORMED BEAUTY

Over the Threshold of joy
Lies the unformed beauty
We are its fingers
Not its touch

A PAINTING

(For Laura Farabough)

The wind pushed us
Through an empty street,
Footless,
The two of us.
And shop keepers
Closed their doors
And were afraid
Of our Silence.

There was no color,
Except for the pale patches of green
Upon your long skirts,
And, of course, the few blue flowers
Strewn between your braids.
They fell,
One by one.
But for all else
There was no color.

— Summer, 1974

POEM FOR MY MOTHER AND FATHER

It is
his vision
which shows me things so small
as to be large beyond measure
It is
her voice
always
in which I hear the music
of unsung poems
It is to them
I return the gift given
with awe full simplicity

— 1977

FRAGMENTS

We
Will lie
In the God
Soft sky,
A piece of
Music worn
By the wind's skin.

CHALON

It was as though
The stars themselves
Were moved by this wind.
And the Wind said,
I make all things clean."It moved
Within the bellies
Of stilled souls
It moved
Through their clear throats
And simple eyes
It moved
Through the breast
Of all living things
Naked, it moved.

It is the music heard by the deaf,
It is the color seen by the blind,
It is the music sung by the mute,
It is the dance where nobody moves.

— Malibu, 1977

EULOGY FOR STUART Z. PERKOFF

The poet lay
Like a fallen tree,
The roots exposed
That ate the earth
In search of vision,
A Holy Greed
For hymns
To feed the mouth
Of hungry heaven.
He lay
With bent limbs
And threw his fist
At the enclosing sky.

And I
Within the closing room
Knelt
In the center of his prayer,
Within its quarrel,
Its refusal,
And heard the waves of poems
In his drowning breath,
And heard
His final poem pressed
Against his throat
Awaiting his surrender
To his muse,
Of she
Who white as breathing
Blew windy poems
Through his open hands.

—Malibu, 1977

REQUIEM FOR A POET

Refuse to sleep,
To be absorbed
By that from which you drank.
Do not go blind and speechless
To that dark and wordless thing.
Heaven's tired
Of it's faint whisperings.
Let it grow loud.

— Malibu, 1977

LITANY (TO THE MUSE)

She is the mountains
Formed by cruel carvings,
Her flesh burns with its bleeding,
Her wounds are blinding,
She has been fed by her nourishings,
Her breasts are stone,
Her rage is solid,
Her touch is not cold,
Her hands reach deep into the earth
To touch the tip of balance.
She listens.
She will be heard.

—Malibu, 1977

A PASSING

It was not a gentle passing
Through the black unbroken air.
It ate us.
It had its stomach full
Of our appetites.
We could not refuse
Its taste.

We were neither asleep nor awake.
The night was blinding.
It held no dream.
Nor was God there.

Our tears became sand.
Our bones thin.
Our souls were without skin.
We did not speak,
But sang our vows of silence.

— Malibu, 1977

WE WAITED ONLY FOR REMEMBRANCE

We waited only for
Remembrance.
We were as open sores
Our hair tangled from our weeping
Our nails torn
We drank little
Our thirst was unquenchable
We sat in the midst of demons
Their gifts of pleasure could not soothe
Our lips were cracked from holy words
That could not be heard
We spoke no more
Our sorrow had left us
Our journey could not be remembered
We could no longer wait
We could only remain.

— Malibu, 1977

PRAYER

I pray
With an ungodly haste
For the Reluctant One
To pour
With scalding force
Wisdom
Which delights itself
In unpossessed motion
And revelation break
Between my palms
With a diamond cry.

— Malibu, 1977

SHE

The white mist
Came over the sea
Like seed
From an unknown god.
While over the smoothe sea
The grey gulls hung
Motionless
In the thick air,
And the soft sea sang
She She She
And the soft sea sang
As they stared at a small child
Curled like a newborn
Pushed from the sea.
She lay
At the edge of the light sand
While the white water
Licked her feet
Like a deer
Over its wet fawn,
She rose,
Unsteady,
Clutched at the white sky
While the wide-eyed gulls
Watched
And the red sun
Poked
Like the fingertip of a divinity
That had punctured the horizon.
And the soft sea sang
She She She.
The evening star was rising.
And the godchild grew
In strength and grace
With white hair
And cool black eyes.
And the smoothe sea was pleased
And the smoothe sea sang
And the gulls eyes asked
"Who is she,
Who is she with hands like feathers
That dip into the wind,
Who is she that moves soft
Through the winged wind?"
And the soft sea sang

And the soft sea sat
Like a grey cat
Stationary as stone
The cat sat,
While the gulls asked
"Who is she
Who caused the Cherubim
To commit sins of envy?"
And the sea sang
She She She
While the moon rushed to meet
The evening star.

And the godchild grew breasts
Small like the swells of the full sea,
And the sea was pleased
And the pleased sea spoke
To the child with the quiet heart.
"Go to the purple mountain
That rests upon the milky sea."
And the godchild whispered "Yes."
Soft as a bird
She whispered "Yes."

And the godchild climbed
To the top of the mountain
And found an altar
With a lamb laying upon it,
While the sea sang
"Offer me.
Offer me."
The restless sea sang.
And the sun became as a wound
Which poured its blood
Into an inflamed sea,
While the evening star pressed
Itself against the sky,
And the moon did not move,
And the god child's heart was still,
And the white lamb looked
With cool black eyes
And the gulls watched the throat
Of the quiet white lamb.
The child said "Yes."
Her sad heart said "Yes."
And the red eyed gulls
With flushed wings

Were thrown against each other
By the blind wind,
And fell like wounded Seraphim,
Burning, burning
And the child became red
As the burning sea while the sea rose and sang
"Offer me.
Offer me."

And the child raised her hand
To open the soft flesh
Of the cool eyed lamb,
And the sea spoke
And the quiet heart heard.
"Take the lamb to your breast
And nurse it.
I want no more offerings
Of blood and death.
I want only offerings
Of milk and life."
And the child's heart was glad
And the child took the lamb
And pressed it to her silent heart
And the sun set
And the wind became still
And the sea became a holy black
And the godchild became black
With the simple black of the simple sea.
And the sea sang
While the gulls moved their heads
Under their wings
And the child placed her head
Upon the sea's black breasts
And slept
A black sleep
A holy sleep
And the sea was with ease
And the easeful sea slept
As its black pulse thundered
Beneath its black breath
As the evening star reached
To touch the tips of the waning moon.

And while the god child slept
A great multitude gathered
To look upon her face
And her only food was air and light

And she delighted in all living things
And someone from within the crowd said,
"Who is she? Who is she?
She has no eyes,
How will she see?
She has no ear.
How will she hear?"
She, whose lips are sealed,
How will she speak?
And yet I have heard her say,
'I am the dreamer of the dream.'"

And another rose and said,
"It is she,
It is she who said,
"Come.'
She said she had been waiting,
And showed me a Church
Where her face turns colors with the sun.
A flame pierced my head
And all I saw and heard
Was white.
She said,
'Come again'
For she had many Churches."

And another spoke,
"I said to her,
'May I come?'
And she looked into the sun
And held my hands loosely
And she filled me with a sea of suns.'

And another said,
"It is she
Who became large and dark
And climbed into the sky,
Her foot the mountain
The moon her eye.
And she heaved
And pushed
A bloodless birth,
A clear light flowed like liquid
Upon our skulls,
So that the word was no longer flesh
But burst between our foreheads
Into sound and light,

And poetry became a pastime for our
children."

And the multitude rose and sang,
And a great hum was heard,
And it sang
Like from the black belly
Of the sea
It sang,
"She is She
She is She
She is She."
And the opened sea was pleased.

And the goddess grew large
And stretched herself upon the sea.
Until she became the sea itself,
And the sea said,
"Memory. Memory."
And someone from within the crowd asked,
"What do you wish us to do?"
And the sea said,
"Keep vigil with the dream."
And the air became thick like honey
So that those who wished to fly could fly.
And someone from within the crowd said,
"In the dream we become as birds."

And the dream had the scent
Of all living things
That were being born and dying.
And her dreamed smelled
Like an open wound,
Red with its bleeding.
But the dream could not see itself
Nor could it see the dreamer.
And the sea said,
"Watch your dream
As you would watch your dying."
And someone from within the crowd said,
"I dreamed I didn't dream anymore."
And they were afraid.

And the goddess grew old
And more beautiful
And her blue flesh loosened
So that her arms spread
Into the rivers,

Her fingers
Into the trees.
And those who saw her
Became sad at her leaving.
And someone from within the crowd asked,
"When will she return?"
And the goddess
From within her slumber
Said,
From within her blind dream
She said,
"When you have heard
Your own blood move
Like wind
Through the mountains,
Then you will hear me.
When you have sensed
The seed released
And felt its nudge,
Then you will feel me.
When you have seen sound and light
Become the same
And its movement stilled,
Then you will see me.
When all you senses
Become but open sense,
Then you will know me."

And the sea
Became as crystal.
And the sea said,
"Memory. Memory."
And the sea was still,
And the sleeping sea said,
"We are the dream awakening.'

Began – Venice, 1976
Completed – Malibu, 1977

1980s
(Early to Middle)

AN ANCIENT RACE OF QUEENS

All thought is memory.
We will not even know
What they will call us.

Where will these words go?
They have no memory.

These words are blind
Through your eyes they see.

***

These poems do not know
Who feeds them.

***

Through your forehead
Our eagles fly.
We are the last thing you hear
Before you die
The sound of air
Against the wings of birds.

One stone can tell
The entire story
Of an Ancient Race of Queens
No longer heard.

Our children became sand,
Our poems dust.
Your feet will recognize our touch,
For when you walk
You walk on us.

—Venice, 1981

I AM THE POEM

I am the poem
My restless light
Burns the stem of memory
Your pulse will feel my heat
Listen to my birth
Slow as the sky
And wide
I crawl
Out of the shape of water
Into the sound of breath
I will end
As I began
Silent as between the stars

—Venice, 1981

ODD PHENOMENON IN AN ABANDONED CITY

My skull is full
With conversations of stars
Dry with the heat of God
I am martyred to an Ancient calm
My breasts are cracked.
They know the wounds of all
Yet I have not fainted
My eyes, no more than holes
Of which there is no bottom.
I will sit until every eye
Will see through them

You who hear these words
Will recognize their touch.
Something in you will remember them.

Behind the seal of sleep
I remember
Sluggish time winds
Around oblivious Eternity
Sand over water
Water over sand
Rome, Troy, the City of Angeles
Exhausted Worlds
A Thunder in the Distance

Your breath will find me
Your eyes, too, will become sand
What lies before you
Is your past
You will see all things
At the same time
And therefore will be blind.
I promise

I have fallen far from thought
I have fallen
I have fallen
To where you and I will untie
The final secret

Time has no purpose
Outside of itself.
It does not matter
That this poem is written

Here there are no eyes
Not mine, not yours
Only a dry planet moves
Beneath my knees
And I
Who once heard children shout
Between the leaves
Still cry.

—1982

PASTORALE

The mountains
Are passionate and still
Wings before flight

Butterflies tumble
In the wind
Joy is available

My flesh
Breasts of birds
Poems come to rest

The shadows of birds
Pass through us
We are sky
We are glass

The shape of poems
The shape of wings
Everything is breath

Our skulls are filled
With the conversations of stars

The heart beats for its own sake
The stars: how to remember them
And not to question

My heart, your heart
The sound of a great sea
My voice, your voice
The one wave
Which will roar
Long after
The last star

A child waves at the sea
The child is gone
The sea is gone
These words are gone

VENICE

(On the poetry wall in Venice, California.)

Venice
Holy Ground
Stained with the blood of poets
City which lies
Beneath the breasts of birds
Guarded by cats
Behind every corner
The Muse, Angel of Surprise
Poems out of pavement cracks

VENICE

(Original)

Venice
Holy Ground
Washed with the blood of poets
What does our flesh conceal?
Our smiles join
The walls are not solid
The air does not close completely
Behind our backs
Something of ourselves remains
The poem has no end

Venice
City which lies
Beneath the breasts of birds
Guarded by cats
Behind every corner
The Muse, Angel of surprise
Poems out of pavement cracks
Listen
From where the voice begins

We are the poem
Our restless light
Burns the stem of memory
Listen to our birth
Slow as the sky
And as wide
We crawl out of the shape of water
Into the sound of breath
We will end as we began
Silent as between the stars

JOHN THOMAS

What was that sound?
John Thomas 30 miles away
Writing a poem

—April 6, 1983

TWENTY YEARS

Twenty years
I have sat by this river
Nothing has changed
Only I laugh louder

—April 6, 1983

DEATH ON THE SANTA MONICA FREEWAY

(March 22, 1983 3:15 PM)

And still
I do not know
What I saw.
Only the colors
Remain
The bright yellow
Plastic tarp
On the pale pavement
Its corners raised
Then
Lustrous black hair
Tangled by the rain
The face – ivory
Features – sculptured
On the forehead
A thin red line of blood

I do not know
What I saw
In her smile
Of death
At that moment
When only I
And other strangers
Knew
At that moment
When death was simple
Separated from sorrow
Its beauty
Without its cruelty

Each day
She comes
Closer, yet
I know her less
The yellow, black
The red
Are more brilliant
Often her face
Becomes my face:

When I first awake
Or after love
When rooms are transparent.

She will never speak
Until my final hour
When the veil recedes
When she becomes
More silent still
And I will understand
Her smile

COLD EYE AT 3 A.M.

Cold eye burning
At 3 A.M.

I did not dream
This poem

This moon

THREE HAIKU

A full moon
The white sea is still
The poet snores

*

A waning moon
The shadow of the bamboo
Moves across our footsteps

*

Five grey moths
Dead beneath the windowpane
No moon

EYES OF A GHOST

Now
Have the eyes of a ghost
The night
Now
It will touch you
The night
A mirror
Feel it, the absence
And what is now
About to be taken

THE HOUR OF THE WORLD

It is difficult to know
The hour of the world
If it is not reached in silence

The eyes
Silent
The lips
Parted
In a smile
Which is silent
The ears
Hear
Things so silent
The breath
The eyes move
But they do not move
They are like silent moons
Imagine the moon
And the lips
A smile which is silent
With only the breath
The breath
Nothing but the breath
The hour of the world
Your hands
Still
They reach in silence
But they do not move
You can be so quiet

YOU AND I NOW LIVING

When I awoke I was saying
"This is the dream I heard
In the distance…"

The moon passes
The moon passes again
We're growing old
So old
The centuries
I thought I was invisible
Our eyes
Colder now than the sea
You and I
Now
Living
So that the dead may talk
To one another

"This is the dream I heard
In the distance."

NIGHTLY VIGILS

These nightly vigils
New moon half moon
White vigils all that is white
Old moon dying moon black moon
Vigils of darkness all that is black

Receive it

Ordain yourself

THE CIRCLE

Beyond your circle
The sound of Hell
Is moving all around you
The Demons
Muttering in their fear
You have no fear
Within the circle
The light, white
Impenetrable
Untrampled by any foot
Not even your own
Utterly alone
You are less than a shadow
You have no fear
Before the celebration
Of what is not seen
You are very small
You will disappear
This fire
This fire
Imagine
To make the stones alive
To walk on fire

ROOMS WITHOUT WALLS

Rooms, rooms
Without walls
Empty, floating
Through flames bedded
In the glass buried
In the mirror
Fire in the water
In your words
More than shadows
Your words
Turn the air
Which is fire
Which is water
Which is a lake
Of fire the burning
Crystal draws your face
But you have
No face your shadow
Burns on the lake
Empty no one here
Time becomes moment
Becomes crystal
You are alone
Yet not, not alone
In the stillness
You burn
Your words
Now have power
Your spell turns the world
You burn

THE CLOSING

The purple curtain moves
Shadows are slow rivers
Nothing else remains
But the hand, the cold hands
Covered with memory
And the smiles that fall
Into the mirror

THE CATS

The cats
Always the cats
Watch us like our own death

A SHADOW

I'll show you something subtle
A shadow upon a shadow

THE MOON

Stone of melancholy
Old stone of wind
It is beautiful, the moon
Utterly alone!

YOUR KISS (WAS IT A KISS?)

Your kiss (was it
A kiss?) was
A hazard:
Lava, cinders.
The night lit up
And all the trees caught fire.

The next kiss
(Was it a kiss?):
Pumice, boulders
And rivers of hot mud
The slopes black red orange
Flow after flow
Wind turbulence
In excess of 100 mph.

Krakatoa, Kilimanjaro,
Kilauea, Mauna Loa,
Vesuvius, the Andes,
Mounts St. Helen and Shasta.
You told me it was poems.
I should have known, John:
Your red suspenders should have
Tipped me off.

I REMEMBER

I remember
I thought I was a cat
Walking by the window
But it was the top of a tree
A slow cat

Underneath the dove's wing is
The color of the sky
Underneath the dove's wing is
 The moisture of the night
I miss you at night, love
I miss you at night when I am asleep
I am moving around because
I am searching for you
But I will not call
(I am Irish
I was born polite)
And all I see is
The pen with which I write
The rope swaying up to the sky.

THREE LOVE POEMS FROM THE JAPANESE

Where can I hide
My love for you?
Not in my braids,
You will loosen them.
My lips-
You will open them.
Heaven and earth are too small.

*

With you
I am a nun again
Without a sound
We sit
Shadows
Cast by moonlight
Through white petals.

*

Idle floating continents
Warming of an ice age
I love your slow ways.

LOVE, YOU ARE GREEN AND DARK

Love,
You are green and dark
The field I walked as a child
Slowly, slowly the snow
My favorite word was
Far, far
And the stars
How I had to close my eyes
Before they came too close
And the snow
You are
Green
Like snow
And far

Love, love
In our solitude
Even the sun will abandon us
Put off the naming of things
We'll do it together

WEDDING POEM

Before the stars were
Frozen into fire
I remember
Your voice grew stronger
I the darkness
Which even then
Could not separate us

Remember
I called you
I said
I will not stand
Without you
Between the cold Seraphim
In that heart
Which could not separate us
In that darkness
I stood beside you

SUMMER '85, VENICE

Summer '85

Venice one hundred degrees
But gas shut off, so only
Three showers in four months.
Car breaks. Job lost
Second car breaks. House lost.
Little sleep, hunger, eating
Surplus food from a home for
Unwed mothers. Frozen burritos
And chocolate milk.
The pawn shop will not accept
Our wedding rings. You say,
"Philomene, I love you
When the troubles come."

Winter '85

Homeless in the Santa Cruz Mountains.
Coldest winter in 50 years.
Matches lit next to the skin
To feel their small heat.
Hair in knots and strings
Clothes nearly so.
The greater our need
The more we are despised.
Rejected, finally
By all but a few. You say,
"My love, look to the irreducible bottom:
We have each other."

THIS IS THE MORNING

This is the morning
I have planned for you
I have rehearsed it
With great aspiration
The blood will come
In short phrases

There is a woman
In one room
The action takes place
Outside

The clock moves very fast
There are cries
There are prayers

There is one man
One room
The action takes place
Outside

They speak

"What do we gain
That we do not already have?
What do we lose
That we have not already lost?"

This is the morning
I have planned for you
The conflict is
Whatever you do is wrong
There is a small complication
We may be killed

The morning is in the time span
Of a week
There are windows
Light continually changes
There is one large clock
Time varies, reverses itself
It is now between 11:35 and 11:38
There is one man

There is one woman
They are the same person
The internal dialogue
Is very good
Description, space
Appear just right
Enigmatic
Awkward sentences, but
The style they are developing
Turns inside out

They ask themselves,
"If we become phantoms
Or are already phantoms
What could contain us?"

The sound of leaves moving
A key in the door
Leaves moving
A key in the door

If I repeat myself
It is because I am haunting
My own body

Incessant monologue
The scent of fear
Long hours of
Looking at the sky

She touches him
She says,
"The surfaces are not strong enough
To contain, to

She touches him

One man
One woman
The same person

Their touch acknowledges
The embarrassment
That they do not know
There are compensations

"Clearly we remember
Traces
We choose
Clearly it is the wrong choice
A grievous mischief"

The plum tree is in bloom
A small breeze blows

Why would we be seeking
If it were not waiting
To be found?

I know what I am looking for
But not its name

They spend the day taking photographs
Of where they are to be buried

Plum blossoms
Blow across the ground Waiting to be found

He touches her
He says
"The surfaces are not strong enough
To contain, to

He touches her

JOHN THOMAS

John Thomas
Critical mass
No larger
Than a
Few miles in diameter
And possibly only
10,000 years old
Even his early poems
Could drive a large
Locomotive

HANDLE THIS, BIG GUY

May I congratulate you
On your pronunciation.
John Thomas.
But I see you
Give yourself
The good lines
In your inconsequential olipsist poem
I intend to hate.

Yesterday, a solar eclipse.
Even as we speak
The buffalo are snaking out of Yellowstone
Heading back
To the Great Plains.

SEDUCTION POEM

Come, my love
Pursued by Muses
You do not believe in
Come, my love
A kiss. I am their small daughter
They wish to taste
Your open mouth
In mine, my love
Come, I am reclining, wretched
Wounded by their crimson morning
Lost in their golden hills
They pipe inept concerts
In imperturbable solitudes
Come, the morning is a wound
Dreaming in confusion
For love of you who disbelieves
We have been awake for hours
Pining. My love, come
My lips are the scarlet dawn
Fury until they meet yours
In my mouth are secrets
The whole of County Cork
The ruins of Persepolis
The very next poem you will write.

No. I will not tell them.
They will be only my lips, love
Not the hills of Antrim.
Not the poets of Lesbos
Only my lips. Yes
When the morning star
Rises, I promise you
Will come
After the kiss
The trembling, drunken green

YOU ARE SLEEPING, MY LOVE

You are sleeping, my love
So I am sleeping
White upon white
Eludes me
This lonely shore

JOHN THOMAS, STRETCHED UPON THE BED

John Thomas, stretched upon the bed
The long sand beneath Ozymandias

John
I cannot sleep
Your beauty has awakened me

A LOVE POEM / A DEATH POEM

The scream
Belongs to no one
It is your scream
The wall
Moves
Yes, alive
With shifting light

A caress caught
Mid-gesture
The sound of footsteps
Caught on the wall
Questions posed
For lengthy evenings

"What are we doing?
Would somebody tell me...."
Of the people watching these words,
You say: "They know who they are."

An eye closes
There are purple flowers
Always purple flowers
Green in the grass
Night so black
You see your face in it
Sky above sky
Black within black

The eye opens
What is this melody?
Mysteries in small places
What is this harp
This angel
In stationary flight?
What is this music
That touches nothing?

The leaves rustle
Is there a storm at sea?
We don't know what we want," you say,
"But we don't want this."

I say,
"I dreamed my genius
And now it is behind me.
God is no more than you"
Then,
Desultory sounds
Choreographed movements.

The sun rises
A drop of water

So small a noise
Or so large a death.
It is very loud in here.
That is, it is, I am
It is very loud in here.

I AM REMINDED IT IS SPRING

Patients in canary yellow hospital gowns.
The cafeteria booths also canary yellow.
The droplets of blood on the floor are robin breast red.
The crash cart outside your room is cardinal red.
Everyone is smiling.
You are tied to a telemeter. Also smiling.
The screen where the motion of your heart is described
Looks like a Japanese landscape. Mount Fuji.
I am reminded it is Spring.
On the echo Doppler cardiogram your heart sounds like a
Cat and dog fight.
You arms are bruised from blood tests. (Tie dyed", you say.
I have never enjoyed your hospital humor.)
You talk of hummingbirds. Promise to buy me a
Hummingbird feeder when you return.
It will be red with bright yellow flowers
The doctor says you will be all right.
The second doctor says you will be all right.
The nurse, the second nurse, the dietician and
The maid tell me you will be all right.
I try to believe them.
I do not cry.
I tell no one.

At home I try to vomit, cannot. Only the motions.
Dry heaves over the toilet.
Doves, pigeons, sparrows outside the window. Spring.
I look for hummingbirds.
I try to write you a love poem, but
It comes back through the page twisting its hands.
There are gaping holes where the words would have been.

REASON IS CRUEL

Reason
Is cruel
Nuance, the terrible facts
Are the greatest liars.
Memory, you will recall:
Not true.
The oldest stories
Have been found to have
No history, and
What happens in between
Logic erases.
Even the end of the world,
As the beginning —
A false poem –
Will leave only you, my love.
No night,
No moon,
Only you.

I AM NO LONGER AFRAID

I am no longer afraid
Of this poem
From which
I will never return

I call myself
Only the words follow me
With each breath

I do not disappoint them

Although they
Brought me here
Their voices die
One by one

Other ruminations
No longer my own
Their thunders
Are
Pleasant enough
As
Strapped
To my pen
I slip
Further

THE POEM TAKES A HUNDRED YEARS TO COME

The poem takes
A hundred years
To come

And then it blooms
At night

The branch almost breaks
Under her weight

She is old
She can bear the loneliness

Although she invented angels
She was driven out of heaven

Are you astonished
By her white mouth?

She will tell you
It is blood
That blood is
The silent country

Its orchards ablaze
With the bleeding

EVERY POEM I WRITE

Every poem I write
Is a suicide

It will say,
"I am your death
Hidden in a spasm
Of clay

Dazzling, ferocious
Now only a
Flame in your hand."

THE HERMIT

The Hermit sits in the center of the stage surrounded by sand. There is one cloud in the sky. The lighting (point of view of the sun) changes slightly through the play as if moving through the day. Occasionally there is the distant buzz of a fly. The Hermit's hair is long and white, covering the stage and flowing over into the aisles. Beside her is a tumble weed.

(Pale morning light)

Hermit: What! I'm here again?

(Why does she come back? Is it small? The scent of orange blossoms? Words? She wishes to re-immerse. So it is memory only? To talk. She loves to talk. What about immobility as a problem?)

Tumbleweed: (Silence)

Hermit: Thank you for pretending to be here.

Does my dying effect the sun?

MY MAXIMS:

The devil possesses
More faith
Than you and I

*

There are bad dreams
For those who sleep unwisely

*

How few days there are
In a century

*

We don't know
Are not sure
Where we dream

*

Push anything to its extreme
It becomes its opposite

*

How close to birth
All this crying

*

Now she is where there
Is no wind

*

Her own tears awaken her

*

Faint tremors

*

You think you exist

*

I awaken to go to sleep

*

She is full of sleep

*

    It is as if the Muse was allowed in once to touch tongues and then, because her fire was too great, was immediately banished to some sort of limbo. We have seen the result: the tapping of her powers without remembering their source.

    Still we are not satisfied. Now the poets themselves must knock out one of her eyes. How impudence thrives! I am surprised that the hot-doggers who participated in the "World Poetry Championship" did not break out in boils and a malodorous jock itch.

    No, boxing gloves are not what is required when we are in the hands of mystery. Poetry is never won, never earned. It is always a gift. And we must approach its luminosity with reverence and what little remains of innocence.

LETTERS TO POPE JOHN PAUL II

I

Your Holiness, Pope John Paul II:
I do not expect you
To remember me
On September 15, 1987
I was on the corner
Of Olympic and Western
I wore a black velvet jacket
And purple socks
It gives me great pleasure
To know at this moment
My letter
Is in your hands
And that
Your benevolent eyes
Follow each humble word.
I am writing
To tell you
That every night
For the past 25 years
I dream of nuns
Chasing me

Your most humble servant,
Philomene Long

II

Your Holiness:
Thank you
For your prompt reply
What a surprise!
You do remember me.
Yes. I have green eyes.
Yes. I had been a nun.
And as you surmised
I did escape
In the middle of the night
Down a mountain side
(At the very moment I
Write this
A large
Fly
Died.
Sliding down
The window
Hitting the sill
Landing with
A loud thump).
No. I do not want
The nuns to leave me alone
I simply wanted
To tell you.
I remain

Your most humble servant,
Philomene Long

III
Your Holiness:

I apologize
For not answering
Your telephone call
Last night

It is just that I
Wish to
Maintain only a
Letter correspondence.

You, too, have dreams
Of nuns chasing you?
I have noticed
Often
With no apparent reason
You grimace
Your eyes become small
Then roll towards
The upper left
And if appropriate
You place your
Hand upon you forehead.

Why?
Do you want them
To leave?

Your least of all servants,
Philomene Long

IV

Your Holiness:

Ask them what they want.
I confess
I do not
I am afraid
They would go away

But for you—
Days as well as nights!?
Holy Father!
I confess I wish like you
When I awake
There would be
Nations of nuns
In the room
With me.

Sincerely,
A prostrate Philomene Long

V

Your Holiness:

PRIESTS!
They want to be
PRIESTS!

You ask my advice,
Your Holiness
My first inclination is
Of course, to agree with you
Yes
They have no beards
They are not fishermen
I understand.
But please give me time on this

As for last night
I dreamed you were
In love with me
And came disguised as a cop.

Most Sincerely,
Philomene Long

VI

Your Holiness:

I accept
Your gracious invitation
To the Vatican
Excellent idea
But I would prefer to arrive on the
Feast of Mary Magdalene

Oh! And I did reconsider
The matter of women as priests
Here is my opinion
Correct. Most of the nuns I've seen
Do not have beards
But they have hearts
And from my vantage point

(Both awake and in my dreams)
Enormous ones
Which was Christ's main point
Wasn't it?

So, yes. They should be priests
I hope this will not cause discomfort
For you at our tea
By the way, I take it with milk
No sugar, and no
No need to be concerned
I won't come with nuns

POEM FOR MY MOTHER

Sometimes I feel I can hear her
When I write a poem

When it ends
She is gone

I am always reluctant
To end a poem

*The Cold Ellison Poems
(1987-1989)*

COLD ELLISON I

"Cold cliffs more beautiful
The deeper you enter
Yet no one travels this road."
-Han Shan, Cold Mountain

In this old cold building
"The Ellison"
In this small dark room
I sit cross-legged
Upon an old stale mattress
The feathers are finally
Leaving my pillow
To rejoin the birds of the air

At least once a month
The upstairs neighbor's toilet overflows
Our ceiling bulges
The walls turn black and green

In this dripping room
All my clothes are torn
Our only guests
The ghosts, the mice
Only dust
Over dog eared books
And drifts of paper
Like dirty snow
My daughter stays away, says
"You were never a model
For a nine to five job."
My son visits occasionally
Long enough to smile
And ask for an aspirin

In this cold room
The window is bricked up
The pipes leak
Puddles always on the kitchen floor
Never any rice in the pot
Once there was a view
A eucalyptus tree, a ghost gum
It was cut down in June

I, who once was proud
That they called me
"The Queen of Bohemia"
Now blush, ashamed
"John Thomas!" I call
"I'm trying to bring myself
Out of something –
To nothing...
I'm going to pray to St. Francis
To embrace this poverty!"

"Pray to embrace silence
We already have poverty!" he says
"Hey. We're doing pretty well
For a tired old man
And a crazy lady...
Tomorrow I'll get you
A crown of rhinestones.
Do I give you enough?"

"John, to have you
For my companion
Through the glass centuries
Your diamond body
Calm, enormous land
This is the only center
That I seek."

At night
The cockroaches come out
They walk across my neck
To get to Masami Teraoka's print
"Zen Monk On A Blue Whale"
Hakuin contemplates death
They take refuge in the Buddha
Little insect eyes. Sad. Sad.
But too many. A thousand at least
So they must die
We'll use the money from
Selling our books of poems
To purchase roach poison

There are no roads
From this cold Ellison
Better sit still
And quiet the ills
Of the mind

I sit high in this old building
Higher yet the sky passes slowly
The birds swirl
Incautious, completely free
I climb the road
To cold, cold Ellison
The road that never ends
"Who can break the snares of the world
And sit with me
Among the white clouds?"

COLD ELLISON II

Two and a half years
(On and off)
Earthquake proofing
The Ellison
Steel blades of
Buzz saws on steel I-beams
Pounding of
Hammer on brick
Hammer on brick
Between the shouts
Rage, rage
Between the shouts
Of addicts and prostitutes
Rage, rage

It is impossible to move
For midst the sand and dust my love
John Thomas is the caliph of Baghdad
The man who refused to travel
Because it would require four hundred
Camels to take his bedside books

All day I dream of being a hostage in Iran
Dim basement
Empty walls
Rent free
Food brought to me
Three times a day
Quiet

Only the muffled
Prayers to Allah
In the next room
Occasionally they whip
The souls of my feet
That's all right
It keeps me awake
Which is more silent than dreams

There in Iran
I would sit cross-legged
Until my legs happily
Fell off
My only request
A blindfold
And ear plugs
I would sit
And not even think
Of Bodhidharma staring at that wall for nine years
He's too loud

COLD ELLISON III

"I used to be fairly poor, as poor goes.
Today I hit the bottom of poverty and cold.
Nothing I do seems to come out right.
Wherever I go I get pushed around."
-Han Shan, Cold Mountain

This month
The Cold Ellison
Brought us the Asian Flu
Too much noise
Too little sleep
Then blasts of cement dust
Last night I coughed for fourteen hours
This building is going to kill me

John coughs from across the musty room
He'll claim: "It is the force behind the heavens"

AH! Great statue of the reclining Buddha!
John Thomas, everyday
Stretched across the bed
Leaning on his left elbow
Writes glowing poems
Among his pillows
Of books and dust

There is not enough dust
In this poem

Another cough from across the room
Then John hums
"Om mane padme
Ho humm...
All the bodhisattvas
Are rolling over
Slapping each other
Over that one
In compassionate mirth!"

Last month
Our ninety-year-old neighbor said
This place depressed her
"Too dark, too dark," she said

"Philomene, You deserve
Better than this."

The year's end has left me
Ragged and desolate

With this dust:
My eyes, black circles
I can no longer read, even short poems
Must sit alone in the dark
Hour after hour

Poetry and religion brought me here

Through this cold Ellison
I journey to the very center

COLD ELLISON IV

*"Living in the mountains,
mind ill at ease,
All I do is grieve at
the passing years.
At great labor I gathered
the herbs of long life;
But has all my striving
made me an immortal?"
-Han Shan, Cold Mountain*

Thank you for pretending
To be here
I do not know but
Have I brought you?
The words must have done that
The silence needs neither
You nor me
It is so deeply
Unreasonable
Even the mice have
Left me, and
My dear departed fly

To have died
And still the living are
Unwilling
To release me
I sit
Cross legged my
Broken, bleeding feet
Once I could have had
Much to say
About them
Left palm upon my right
Thumbs touch at the tips
Is this my hand? Or a
Cloud? I hear my own
Weeping in
The distance
Their laughter
Over my grave
My hair was once
A brilliant red

Or yellow? Everyone said so
My eyes, I think, were green
The sand has scraped
The color from them
Eyes now white
Hair white
So much hair, and
Each strand causes me pain

Am I here then?
I can scarcely hear
My own words
Or yours
This endless yawn and gape of sand
Exhausts me
Once I had hoped
(Was this vanity?)
For my death
To be worthwhile, not
To become simply sand
More sand

Thank you for pretending
To be here

COLD ELLISON V

Warm summery days
At the Ellison
And "Bones" the young dog Chris found
In the last stages of starvation
Infected with heartworms
Damaged eye from being kicked
Back full of gun pellets
And Chris had to carry him everywhere
Slung across his shoulders like a mink stole
It was beginning to seem that
He was deciding he would spend
The rest of his life on Chris' shoulders.
"Bones" is fat now, and trots

Fat lazy days at the Ellison
And the building is finally earthquake proof
So that with the 7.5 sent from Joshua Tree
And the 3,000 aftershocks
It moved with such grace
Cruised the shocks, the ripples
Like an elegant ship
And it still moves
To the music in Paul and Barb's apartment

And for my son Patrick
(My beautiful son)
And the Blue Crew surfers, these days
The waves are good
At night I walk down to the sea
And in the very place
They ride their boards
Dolphins leap and roll and ride
The waves in themselves
The very spot
Must be a good one
Warm summer waves

Soft swaying days
At the Ellison
Its marshmallow bricks
The lazy elevator
And my daughter Maureen returns
From Asia (my beautiful daughter)

She brings me a gift
Of a Buddhist Temple bell
The bell she gives me
Brings three dreams —
I dream I am a Buddhist monk
And that I have been given
A small Zendo
The size of our apartment
I dream I enter a deep dark cave
Where there are Giant Living Buddhas

I dream I am a
Buddhist monk basketball team
But they have to stop the game
Because we are jumping too high

"Now that's a the real dream team"
My daughter says

Soft summer days
At the Ellison
John whispers
Across the room

"You and I, Philomene, that's
All that matters —
You and I"

"You and I, John and
The radiant, the vast..."

"Apartment", he says

Soft, dreaming days
The Ellison dreaming, swaying
Dipping and sailing
Its own warm seas

COLD ELLISON VI

"As for me, I delight in the everyday way,
Amidst wrapped vines and rocky caves.
Here in the wilderness I am completely free."
-Han Shan, Cold Mountain

Silver days at the Ellison
Longest rainstorm in ten years
Beneath the slippery sky
The Ellison glistening
Dangling raindrops
Silver sounds

Sunset
I slip out to the sea
I am the only person
On Venice beach
Grey sea, grey sky, grey sea gulls
I am wearing a bright pink raincoat
The seagulls believe I am the sunset
They turn their backs to the sea and face me
They assume their sunset viewing positions
Chests forward
Motionless. Except for
An occasional scratch of the ear
The flutter of a wing

We watch each other
I act like the sunset for them
I raise my glowing pink arms
I stand motionless for a long time
Kneel, then recline upon my heels
Alone on Venice Beach
It is all so slow, so simple
Being a sunset

Back at the Ellison.
Alone at the black iron gate
I look up
Soft rain sliding
Over the red bricks
Two red brick wings open
As if to embrace me
Two ghostly shimmering red wings

We watch each other
I look at the Ellison
As the sea gulls looked at me
I love this old building!
I love this old building!

Ah! yes, Kukai, the gulls and
Yes! Even these stones
Will become Buddhas

COLD ELLISON VII

This is a dynamic account of
Blinking and breathing
At day the pigeons outside the window
Eye our apartment with envy
At night I haunt the Ellison
In long white gowns, white veils
At dawn, more pigeons
Then arriving gloriously with the sun
Flies from a living mobile
In the center of our room

Photographs of dead Zen saints surround us
On the wall, a large wooden crucifix
Holy water, oils and two white candles
Within it. Portable for the rite of the dying
It is the last thing I see each night
Before I go to sleep

The landlord is running from
The law. On sight they can
Arrest him for what he's done
To this building.
John Thomas calls him a devil
"What this building needs," he says
"Is an Exorcist."
Never before have I had the law
On my side, not even
The Ten Commandments

Last night Harry Northup
Kindly found us someone
Who would clean our apartment
For only twenty-five dollars
But I didn't have the heart
To tell him we won't
Have that kind of money
For six months

Last night Holly Prado told us
"That you love each other,
That you live in this tiny apartment
Is a miracle."
This morning another spiral of flies
The pigeons blink and breathe

It is good that I hung
That picture in the kitchen
Where they bricked up the window —
The woman with long auburn hair and crown
Ascending, chains breaking from her wrists
Angels circling. It reminds me of my future—
To be crowned in Heaven. That I was once
Crowned there already, that...

"John," I shout from across the room
"You said you would get
My Queendom back for me!"
"I have," he says
"What do you call this!"

"Queen of Bohemia!
 Now Queen of Leaks!
Queen of Pigeons!
Queen of these catacombs!
John, you're making me feel
Like this squalor is better than Heaven!"
"It took you eight years to
Realize that!" he says

The pigeons have mastered their envy
And settled for our windowsill
Their orange eyes radiantly blinking
Golden crown
Celestial pigeons

The California Mission Poems

INTRODUCTION

The intention of the Padres was to bring new life to the native Indians, then to return to them the cultivated mission land. In the end, the Indians' culture was erased, the Indians themselves were destroyed by disease, and their land was confiscated by settlers and politicians. Little remains of the heroic efforts of both Padre and Indian but the mission buildings themselves, and a reverent memory of what has been called a "noble failure.

The Padres cut crosses
On the oak trees to mark
Their path north.

They also sowed mustard seed.

The yellow blossoms of wild mustard
Showed the way from afar along what
Would become El Camino Real.

The life of the Indians was
Changed forever.

They are buried now in their
Thousands, near the bones
Of the Friars

Little remains but the
Buildings they raised
Up together.

JUNIPERO SERRA

The
Blessed
Padre
Who
Once
Walked
Under
Our
California
Sun
Now
Travels
Another
Golden Country.
We continue
To be
Illumined
By his
Bright Shadow

LA PURISIMA

I am not here
Bent, brittle
Weed among weeds
Not here
Palms fragrant with lavender
Hair meandering through
The pale grasses
I can no longer remember
I preferred all martyrdoms
To this dry, silent place

There were nights when I feared
My own blood. My eyes
Became wounds. They devoured
Me. And the flies. Ten thousand
Tangled devils. My palms scoured
Dry and thin as communion wafers.

There were nights when the hymns I sang
Became the bones of the Friar, the dust
Upon the graves of stillborn Indians
The winds of La Purisima
Through the pale grass
I can no longer remember

SAN JUAN BAUTISTA

Behind broken gates
Gray arcades
Golden Spanish reredos
The walls hold them
These voices, resplendent
Crying, chanting
Now mute
Clouds over the valley
Of San Juan Bautista
Blue hills, yellow poppies
Bronze skin, silver voices
The bells could be heard
For fourteen miles
Along El Camino Real
This California wilderness

SAN FERNANDO MISSION

Green the hours
Measured by bells
The sound of water
Twenty-one adobe arches
Fountain the shape
Of a flower
Young grass
Over old graves
Green the shadows
Of Franciscan Friars

Green the doors opening
To all thirsty travelers
Then, now, and after

CARMEL

A memory
Shaped from adobe
And stone
Patches of grass
On a blotched ochre wall
A murmur

Is it the skewed star window
Or the unmoving bell?
A murmur. A presence

Serra
Crespi
Lopez
Lasuen
And in the tiny graveyard
Three thousand Indians

A pepper tree
Leans over their graves
Reaching
As if to touch them
Cannot
As we cannot

This Mission of Carmel
This host of lives
Like the Eucharist Itself
Astound

MISSION SAN DIEGO DE ALCALA

Born of
Fire and blood
Even the earth
Rejected you
Floods, too many tremors
Then abandoned

Still
The serene white façade
And from the arched doorway
Pale scorched walls
Open like arms
In a stylized gesture
Of welcome

Mission San Diego de Alcala
Mother of Alta California
Under the continuing
Blue skies
How slowly
You move
Through the silence

MISSION SAN ANTONIO DE PADUA

The olive tree
Planted beside
The campanario
Its seed, placed
In the earth
Two hundred years ago
Still grows
The desire
Of Father Junipero
That this bell
Might be heard
All over the world"

Mission San Antonio
Planted at the base of
A tower of silence
Not wide but of
Enormous weight
It rises
Straight up, a column
Of infinite distance
To God
Who perhaps only
Touches us
In the stillness of
These tall and ringing
Tunnels

SOLEDAD

(Nuestra Senora de la Soledad)

Soledad. Solitude.
Rumbles walls, winds
Husking through the empty arches
Bitter Land baked dry
Cattle bones drying to chalk
On the grassless plain
Adobe to brown mud to
Dust

By the end thirty padres
Had come, had lived in
Cold and damp
With aching bones then
Hunger, thirst, and bitter loneliness
Puzzling the Indians
While the cattle starved

Prayers, the hollow echoes of prayers
Hunger, night of horrible dreams
The scholarly and amiable
Sarria was the last. Watched
By the puzzled Indians
He starved, collapsed right before the altar
Died

This is the mournful ruin
This is the bitter ruin
This is the unanswered prayer
Named, for once, by the Indians
Named Soledad

SAN MIGUEL MISSION

10,000 years. 500 tribes and tribelets
Now almost nothing remains
Blue glass beads
Embedded in clay
Footprint of an
Indian child
Pressed in homemade Spanish tile
No names
Above their graves,
The very tongues
In which they spoke
Now lost

"Everything in this world talks
Just as we are talking now,
The trees, rocks, everything.
But we cannot understand them
Just as the white people
Do not understand Indians."

They named the birds
In imitation of their call.
They painted their own flesh
Yellow, white, red
Painted the walls
Of Mission San Miguel
Painted that bright
All-seeing eye

"The rock says, Don't.
You are hurting me!
The tree says, Don't.
I am sore. Don't hurt me.
But they chop it down
And cut it up.
The spirit of the land
Hates them."

Almost nothing remains
Rattles made of pebbles
In dried cocoons
Bird-bone-whistles
Small splay-toed food print

The All-seeing eye still ablaze
Above the statue of St. Michael
No names above their graves
Almost nothing remains

"We are not like the mountain
We are not like the sky
Always there
Not like the sun or moon.
We die."

MISSION SAN LUIS REY

San Luis Rey was built under the guidance of the exceptional Padre Peyri. After secularization, the Padre left to return to Spain. Many of the Indians swam towards his departing ship to plead that he not leave them, only to receive a final blessing.

It has its own mind, the past
Which is unreadable
One can never know
Which are the rewards
Which the punishments
Is even a false cross
The True Cross?

A few images remain
Mission San Luis Rey
Lone white tower
Set back on a low hill
Corridors wine red
In its cruciform church
That dome, which is a bell of light
In a dark cubicle
An old Franciscan robe hangs
His broad brimmed Spanish hat
His rosary

Tower, dome, the cross
Weeping Indians, arms extended
Wading into the sea
Padre Peyri's desolate blessing
All a kind of permanent gesture
As if wanting to call for something
Call to something
And not to know its names
Or ours

SAN JUAN CAPISTRANO

A door opened
Then closed forever

Old stones gathered
And fit into place
By the Indians
Ivy covered walls
Twisting ropes of
Rose vines
Moss over fountains
Indians, faded, lost
In Pacific mists
The hauntings
Of swallows
Cold knife of this world

San Juan Capistrano
Slowly fading pulse
Of the cut flower
Two bells toll
One says ever
The other says never
The hauntings
Of swallows
Wave after wave
We twist helpless in
The beak of time
Waiting our time

Mass for the Dead

INTROIT

Silence drifts down
Upon silence, doors
Stop all questions

Born from the mouth
Of the dead
Tall, the ghosts
Tall, the wind
That wraps round
Our sorrow
This marble tomb,
Our sky, opens
The wound each day

Shadows carved by night
Shadows that weep
Upon each born
Below the surface
Of light

Miserere nobis
Dona eis pacen

GRADUAL

The darkness
Which covers the earth
Is terrified
Has no bright wings
To feel the warmth
No tears
To praise it

Et lux perpetua luceat eis
May perpetual light
Shine upon us

EPISTLE

Scribe: Beati mortui
Write: Blessed are the dead

GOSPEL

I heard a voice saying
"I have built
A fire
From your ashes."

COMMUNION

Within this darkness
The light
Within its silence
The cry
Within the cry
Memory

Within the dead
Memory

POST COMMUNION

May we
See with their eyes
As they always
See through ours
As these words
Are their words
Before us
Within us
Now
The bright shared
Countenance
In saecula saeculorum
Forever and ever
Without end
The Radiance

Ireland Poems

IRELAND

(For the Coghlans of County Cork)

Ireland
Whose warriors fought
Their battles naked
Whose Queens waged war with music
Cast spells of ink about the isle
Black fogs to blind
Invaders form the sea

Land which haunts
Its own ghosts
Mists
Sad vapors
Lost poems
Through Tara's halls of gold
Ruined harps
Their broken strings
Tangled
In the grass blades
The violent green memories

Ireland
Her daughters
Her sons
The land
The blood
One thing

Intimate blade
Which inhabits the body
Moss buried
In the flesh
In their eyes
The silhouettes of horses
Dreaming the soft green air

STONE CIRCLE OF DROMBEG

(County Cork, Ireland)

Black rock
Of carefully placed tears
Shafts
Of ancient wind and melancholy
Silhouettes
Of Erin's memory
Stones
Teaching the grass

Great blind masts
Cast upon a passionate green tide
Voyages
In an empty room
Shadows of rites
Imitating water
Imprisoned in stone
Ghosts
Pinned by the weight of stone
Fierce green deaths

Statues
In flight
Inky lashes of the night
Dusty eyes
Of stone
Portraits
That do not reply
Unfinished conversations
Fingers
Rising
From the moss

Relics
Of stone words
Rooted echoes
Of a Bronze Age eloquence
Dreaming in the green morning
Long ardent conversations
Of stone

God's dust
Stone circle of Drombeg
Eloquent hinge
The earth swings
And we enter
The great blind doorway

GRASS, STONE, WIND

Erin
The land itself
A phantom
Of stone and grass
As if dropped
From the sky
From what of rain?
What mystic's ecstasy
In stone?

In the abandoned monastery
Of Bally Beg
What chorus of grass?
At Mallow-
The ruined Gothic Church
Where now
Only cows graze
While from the ruins
At Buttevant
Stones gaze
Almost longingly
At the new church

From what stern night
Celtic crosses strewn
Across Erin
Like stone blades,
Wind into stone

And stepping solemnly
Through another ruin,
Geese. Whose ghosts?
And there a crow
Where once croaked
A Mother Superior,
Where once prayer
Was sung
Now, the sweet wind
Or is it only wind?
Wind into stone
Into grass

Grass
Over Erin's first dead
Queens over warriors
King over king
The gilded dead
The clamorous dead
Druid beside Viking
Anglo-Norman
The grass received them all
The gentle unfortunate
Poet queen
The murdered monks and scholars
The blood ran
The blood ran
The land was drenched
With this blood
The land burst
Into tears
Mist rising
From the grass

Grass into
Wind into Stone.
Stone sky
Gray sleep

THE TALL TOWERS OF IRELAND

The whistling winds
Threads them
With tales of sea-robbers
In dragon ships
Old tales, weary tales
These sad gray
Flutes of stone
They beg the wind
To be done with them
Beg the grass
To cover all

Late 1980s

THE FLOWERS: ARE THEY TRULY EVIL?

I must speak softly
The flowers:
Are they truly evil?
This Spring
There is a
Soundless violence

There is no question
They began us
We only breathe
To feed them

They had already
Warned us
(Venice Fly Traps-
Have you ever seen a
Mouth so red?)

And now they have coated
Their seeds (the red ones)
With poisonous slime
To make themselves immortal

They're going to take it all back
As they should

THAT'S IT! JOHN AND I ARE PACKED

Now we need
(In Okefenonkee anyway)
Written permission
To touch and alligator
Soon it will be the trees

That's it!
Besides, John and I are packed
Having already made plans to leave

OLD FOOL!

Old fool!
I missed
The meaning
Of snow—
Its nakedness

ATRIAL FIBRILLATION

(For John Thomas)

Atrial Fibrillation
Beautiful term
Could be the title of
An obscure but
Marvelous piece by Bach

Atrial Fibrillation
Sounds like
The name of the woods
You roamed as a child
Silver trunks of dead, blighted
Chestnut trees
And incandescent streams

WHISPERS

Tonight's thin fog
Whispers
From a tiny crypt
In search of eulogies

I, TOO, DIED

With my hands in the snow
White
The earth
My hands

I have not named it yet
It has the quality of a cat's eye
Turns in the light
Gives the illusion of depth
Becomes invisible
The sky
Black
The earth
My hands

WEDDING POEM FOR RACHEL AND MARK

Dry, dry and
sharp
all points
and
blades
on an
empty
desert
slope
alone for
(they
say) a
century
then
from
the
center
this
tall
shaft
leaps
as it
were
in (it
seems)
just
days

Pale green, perfect, balanced
in the dry desert air and
at the top, the small golden flowers.
Rachel. Mark. Your Wedding Day.

— Philomene Long / John Thomas

IMMENSE RED ROSE OF BEIJING

Even if it lies
Impotent, a mere word
On the white page
I have a horror now
Of the color red
Even to pronounce it
For a moment
To hold it in my body
A part of my breath

Red night
Immense rose opening
I cannot stop
Their slaughter
Immense red rose of Beijing

HE WAS CHOKING ME

He was choking me and
Pulling my face off it
Didn't hurt I just hated
The skin separating from
The bone it was more the
Idea of my face coming out that
Was bad then he
Opened the back of my head
With the point of
An ash tray there was
Blood coming rather calmly
Out of my mouth
At Bellevue the police
Urged me to press charges
I said no.
It would ruin his reputation, I said.

18 years later on the other side of
The country a woman told the police
He was threatening her and
Filed a complaint
He said she
Ruined his reputation
And sure enough, he
Hanged himself.

WHY I DO NOT READ THE LA TIMES

I have the Irish taste
For melancholy
Therefore, I will not read
This morning's newspaper
Color of dust and sand and
Funeral ashes
Ghostly ancestors
Who wrestle with
Their own angels.
Yesterday
Folded on the doorstep

More will live
Than have died. There is
More future than past, but
Newspapers have little to do
With it
The sand less

Neptune fades slowly from the news
Everything erases itself and
To the angels all our words
Must sound like clichés

PLANT III

(Given to me by Ellen Mitchell)

My little Buckaroo
To me, dear
You will always be
As I first saw you)
The flowering
Of Dante's Final
Paradisiacal Circle
Although now
You take on
More the appearance
Of your birthright:
A Cabbage

Nowadays you look
More like
What you really are:
A cabbage,
But for me you are always
As I first saw you:
The flowering of Dante's
Final celestial circle

SAN FRANCISCO EARTHQUAKE

October 17, 1989 5:04 P.M.

The earth is not
A refuge
It trembles
Opens

From beneath
The Nimitz rubble
That tomb
Of deepest black
Deepest peace
Hands grope
For what is most familiar:
The unattainable sky

The earth is not a refuge
It opens
Seizes us

Sealed walls
Half-closed eyes
Smeared images
Broken air
Final cries
Shot into the dark
Clenched fingers
Now dreaming
In a closed book

The earth is not
A refuge
It opens, seizes us
Folds

This October
The land is again
As the sea and sky
Have always been –
All smoke
Vast emptiness

THE MOTH

(In Panama there are moths that live solely on tears; the tears of large land animals.)

The poem comes
Its currents brush
My lips
Even in sleep
I want to stay near
To what I fear, near
Enough to keep
An eye on it.
I awake
Feel it on my fingertips
Try to clutch it
Before it darts away.
Cannot.

This morning
In the room
A poem, wings beating
John Thomas
Snatches merely
A hot fragment
Before it is gone.

Stuart Perkoff
His voice darkening, died
With the unwritten poem
Fluttering in his fist
Two hours later
I bent to kiss his face
Felt the heat of it
Still on his forehead.

Asleep, awake
Even in our deaths
I suppose the poem
Does not need us
Holds its own bright secrets
To itself
Knows it is finer
Than all these lines
Of iridescent wing dust, pale ash

THERE IS NO COMFORT

There is no comfort
In the poem
Expect to be seared
But to have entry

There are always
The rains
They leave no survivors
The poem's ocean is stone

Who knows
What god will be found in its ashes

There is calm
In the power of its snows
I speak for the dead

1990s

VENICE WOMAN TOSSING TERRA COTTA PLANTER, HITS GUNMAN

Fawn Walenski's aim is a true as her love."—The Santa Monica Evening Outlook

"Mind my bullet wound."
I've just finished hugging Fawn Walenski because I love her.
It is the first time I have ever heard those words—
"Mind my bullet wound."
Before she would explain she needed one more word
To complete her acrostic puzzle.
"What is a four letter word for Zen paradox?" she asked.
"Koan," I answered.
Now, this is her story as I understand it:

At the door of their basement apartment in Thornton Tower
The gunman hollers,
"GIMME ALL YOU GOT! I AX YOU GIMME ALL YOU GOT!"
Jonathon Thays replies,
"I've got a dollar."

In the narrow basement hall
Gray white walls, one bald light bulb
Fawn watches from the door—
Jonathon, his cold cheek against the cold cement floor.
His eyes become blank as the beginning of time.
The only color, the blue of Fawn's t-shirt
With REO SPEEDWAGON written in bold print.
"Go inside, " Jonathon tells Fawn, thinking only of her,
The barrel of the gun now at his head, execution style.
Fawn goes inside. She closes the door.
The image of his face is before her.
"Like a lamb led to the slaughter," she thinks.
"Gentle innocence."

Then she sees a planter of terra cotta,
The one she had been trying to give away to everyone
Even to me, the last time I saw her.

She picks up the terra cotta planter,
Feels the silky smooth cast of the pot,
Knowing it could cut like a knife.
She has never felt such peace,
Not even when she cleaned the church until it crackled.
"I can do this," she says. "I can do this."

She opens the door.
She sees the gunman's foot against the small of Jonathon's back,
The finger tense around the trigger.
Her fingers loose around the terra cotta.
She has never felt a cast so smooth.
Her balance is perfect.
She has no fear.
"I'm not going to let you hurt him," she says.

The gunman turns, aims at Fawn's heart.
Again, she says, "I'm not going to let you hurt him."
Her hair is the color of terra cotta,
Through her throat a tawny river of lions flows.
The gunman, his eyes are like startled mice.

The terra cotta released becomes a stampede of red hot horses,
Becomes a thousand lilies on fire,
A long thin wind of flame,
Which follows her gaze, its blade, a ruby red.
On her fingertips the light is solid.
In her right eye she sees the graceful terra cotta
Hit the gunman's shoulder.
In her left eye she sees the flash of his gun.

The bullet which pierces her chest
Moves like a skipping stone through her flesh.
As if unwilling to harm her
Avoids even the smallest of her bones
Darts past her heart, her lungs
Vaults out of her back to shatter
Only the plaster behind her.

Later she will suspend an empty picture frame
Around the bullet hole in the wall,
Receive the Carnegie medal for heroism
(That year only eight would receive it in America),
And with the award money buy exercise equipment.
And she will give me a fragment (this time I will take it)
Of that clay planter which now happily sits
On my altar upon the Buddha's lap.

But what happened to the gunman?
And what did he do with his dollar?
He picked the wrong immortal couple,
The wrong terra cotta.

A VOICE FOR THOSE WHO HAVE NO VOICE

El Salvador November 16, 1989

In the forests
Of Central America
Lives the Quetzal,
A bird
With iridescent feathers.
It is of
Extraordinary beauty.
They are so rare
That to shoot them
Is illegal
They shoot them anyway

Down the steps
Around the corner
Disappearing
Into the walls
Here is where
The shots came from
There was no wind
To carry their cries
Then the sunrise
Found their blood
Made it incandescent

Awakened now
To a deeper sleep
The priests
Lie almost tenderly
Upon their ground
Journalists and clergy
Surround them, stare
Take pictures
Awkwardly offer prayers

Felled, broken
The priests are mute
Yet in their deaths
A still finer eloquence
El Salvador is
Far away
But not too far
For us to hear
Their high and lonely call

CEMETERY IN THE SAND

(A nursery rhyme for my son during the Persian Gulf War)

Between the death
And the weeping
The flies alone
Are well fed

I am told we can kill them
Two hundred of them
In one second
Two hundred
The age of my son
Nineteen, twenty, twenty-one
They crawl on all fours
Crying for home

Two hundred a second
Too many to place gently
Each in the ground
Dumped two, three, four
At a time
Not even a body bag
Between them and the earth
On the sand
Others strewn
Belching
As they decay
Into withered rocks
Hard black mummies
In oversized clothes
Lying in patches
Of their own grease

Before the death
There is a moments' release
The fleas leave
But then the rats come

The infinite sadness of the world
Is the death of its young

But the dessert will comfort them
Sand

Buried in their flesh
In their eyes
Nothing grows
And all that is left
Is sand upon sand
Like a hand
Settled gently upon them forever
While above –
The silhouettes of rusty canons
Dreaming in the black air

PALACES AND COLONNADES

"Palaces and colonnades, cities
Neither wholly real nor
Wholly in the mind."

But I am she who will always
Find you tracing the elusive future
Tracing the path left in the air

By tomorrow's butterfly
Through the ten thousand seasons
Of sand

MEMOIRS OF A NUN ON FIRE

"You are worldly, Sister Marie Philomene,"
the Mother Superior had said in the parlor
bent over me, tall, angular, aristocratic
like the silhouette of a praying mantis.
"Even your voice, its inflections. Worldly."

At that I was to kneel on the spot.
Kneel with no excuses.
Blind obedience.
Drop to the floor like a swatted fly.

Eyes lowered, lips closed.
I wiggled. My veil fluttered.
My knees bent a little, then locked.
I would not.

Back straight, head erect,
my eyes wide, cool, and I hope vacant,
I stared into her triangular face. I turned. Left
through the dim corridors of no time or season.

In my room I reached through the silence, and
as if from a great height,
watched my hands take the scissors,
begin to cut name tags off veils,
stockings, underwear.
Everything.
All over the room,
threads and scraps of my name,
"Sister Marie Philomene" like tiny white clouds
far beneath my feet.

I knew I would leave that night.
Just walk out.

Five years within this cloister.
An enclosure of silence.
Latin. Eyes fixed to the floor.
Black robes, medieval gestures.
In the most secret recesses,
a thousand daily deaths.

At the end of the hall the life-size crucifix.
Christ's bruised knee,
the level of our lips.
A well-kissed knee.
Through these corridors
we glide through our own ghosts.
Muted light. Fluid movements.
Everything clean. Silent and clean.
"I have loved, O Lord, the beauty of Thy house."

But here some things feel dirty.
Like in my dreams.
In the convent I do not dream of the good sisters.
Each night it is a dark man who follows me.
He is tall, thin, and wears black. All black.
His half smile is repulsive.
He wants to kiss me. Every night in my dreams.
Sometimes he removes my veil,
runs his fingers through my hair.
Once he does kiss me.
I am frightened. I tell another sister.
She says the dark man is myself.

And then— the night I was seduced
by God disguised as a fat black fly.
As a Bride of God I was told to experience the Mystical Union
I must make my mind empty, an erased blackboard.
I contemplate the blackness of space,
the millions of light years between the stars.
I stretch my mind until it is no longer fixed anywhere.
I became the Bride of the Expansive Black.
I kiss it. Marry it. Its deep silence.
But it is difficult to contemplate the Immensity
while enduring a small but persistent itch.

Daily I work shoveling the convent's garbage into the incinerator.
The flies and yellow jackets are very friendly.
At times the golden insects cover my black serge habit
like a jeweled mantle, as the flies circle my head.
At first I do not know that one fly has crept into my ear to rest.
I suppose it has awakened, confused, and is trying to escape.
Lost deep within my ear canal, it buzzes with mounting intensity.
Its buzz is as loud and wide as the universe I am contemplating.
Finally, I know it is not God, but only a fly.
Or is it God disguised as a fly? Is it the buzz of God?

Not only is it a hot summer day, but I am having my period.
I begin to twitch and squirm on the sanitary napkin.
The fly buzzes with growing desperation.
My twitching on the pad increases.
As the fly's delirium grows, so does mine
given the heat, the perspiration,
the itchy habit, the sanitary napkin, and
the frantic buzzing of that fly. That Fly?
When it emerges into my outer ear
I open the side of my head gear and the fly flies out.
At this moment, this very moment, I have my first orgasm.
I know what it was because
I have felt the sensation begin once before
while kissing my high school sweetheart.
While I bounce on the pew, I see it at the corner of my eye
an enormous black fly.
It hangs in mid-air as if to look at me for a moment.
The most beautiful fly I've ever seen.

But what did the nuns see as they sat silently behind me-
everyone motionless except one bouncing nun and
a hovering fly beside her?
I will never know. No one ever mentions it.
No one ever mentions anything personal.
And if they do, what would they say,
"Excuse me, Sister Marie Philomene,
but did I see you having an orgasm
during five o'clock meditation?"

*

Beat. Beaten. Beatific.

I am on my knees before the bed, the crucifix.
This particular night is exceptionally dark.
It is this night I am to understand I am a poet.

Saturday night. Time to whip ourselves again.
I wonder is Cardinal McIntyre doing this?
But I will do it right this time.
Five years within the convent and I have not yet done it right.
Each time the hand that holds the chains has exerted its own will.
I say to the night, "I will tonight. I will beat myself until I bleed."

My body, mind – one thing.

I raise the chain high up. Higher.
That way it will come down with greater force –
to beat, beat. To beat, to be beaten. Higher. Faster.
Body, mind, chain – one thing. One will.
To strike repeatedly. To beat to blood.

It ends.
I run my fingers over my back.
There is blood.
For the first time – blood.
A small amount. But I did it.
"Beautiful blood," I say.
I remove my habit.
I run my fingers over the spot.
Yes. It is blood.
Beatific blood. Beatific spot.
Slowly, I turn in awe to see it.
It, indeed, is beautiful.
But it, my beatific spot...
is a mosquito bite!

I stand in the center of the room. Let loose a mighty laugh.
"Beatific mosquito! Beatific bite!"

I, who have been the Bride of flies,
have become the Bride of mosquitoes.
"Holy proboscis! Probe of fire!"
(Didn't Saint Rose of Lima, out among the mosquitoes
so that they might bite her, say their hum sounded to her
like a choir of angels?)

"O Holy Night! The mosquitoes are quietly biting.
Little fly. Great night."

If you would have looked into this dark corner,
you would have found Philomene naked as if by the night,
a Philomene who no longer hid her heart under crossed arms,
but who excitedly held her breasts in her hands as if
she were offering them to her beloved.

Hers was a song of...
No, it was deeper even:
it was a prayer, as the priest mutters
from the altar holding up the Host.
Her heart thumping in this forgotten corner as she prayed.

You would see her dare to look at her own body,
in the stark black night.
Her body, golden serpentine,
glowing cheeks, glistening eyes, crimson tongue.
In this night of black finger, her slick long body rising,
rising in the blackness – slowly, very slowly turning,
turning in the unseeing dreadful hole of night.
The night, its burning lips, the night of kisses.
She danced. Naked burning bride of God.
In the Grand Silence, you could hear Philomene whisper,
"I am a poet."

But I will always be a nun.
Always in my dreams I am a shabby nun.
There are flies under my habit
and my robes are in bits and pieces.

I will always have a preference for the extreme.
Even now I prefer the company of a St. Francis of Assisi
taking his clothes off in public,
or St. Simeon Stylites
who sat for years atop a high column,
or St. Joan of Arc
who heard voices and dressed in men's clothes.
Even now I prefer to live among
the poets, saints and mad ones of Venice West.
I know no other way but to strip and leap naked
into the Holy Fires.

Burn. Burn. Must burn.

L.A. RIOT POEM

(Venice, April 30, 1992)

Today Venice is
A mysterious, a lonely, a solitary
And indeed, a most ghostly place
Green is the color
Of the stifled air
Along the promenade
The terrified palms.
Only the gulls are at ease
They have their city back

Along the shore
At the high tide mark
a lone of black ash
And red dead Lady Bugs
Thousands of them
Their black wings splayed
In death
Only one is alive
I sing to it.
"Lady Bug, Lady Bug
Fly away home.
Your house is on fire
Your children are alone."

The earth's crust feels
Thinner today
As the sun sets
L.A. disintegrates
In all the morbid shades
Of a fading bruise
This crimson dusk
This amber moment
Los Angeles burning
The walls cave in
The creatures perish
In their cages
The names of the dead
Rise like mist
From the bare ground

It seems to me

We cannot keep the common story
Struggling, straining every second
To keep the sky above us
To keep the sun in the sky
To keep the dead in the earth
To keep all things
So to speak, where they belong
What a crushing task!

II

I return from the sea
Curfew
John sits before the television
John Thomas, like a Giant Panda
Wise in his sloth
The man who has failed
To place himself in life
Success of a sort
He sits in the rocking chair
And quotes L.M. Boyd:
"Ninety-nine percent of the universe is nothing."
"There will be no riot in Venice tomorrow," he says

"Yeah," I say, "if you stay in bed."

"Which is where everyone should be anyway
The best riots are in bed" he says

"No riot? What do you find lacking?"

"Variety, persistence. They are a bunch of amateurs."

"Compared to you, Hotspur. What would you do for a riot?"

"I would give the news helicopters advance notice
As to what intersection it will be— then pull
Arnold Schwarzenegger out of his Mercedes
And club him with Sylvester Stallone."

On the television, Los Angeles
Its sky the same color as smoke

"I tend to take the cosmic view," he shrugs
"If one accepts the current opinion on these matters...
After the Big Bang everything seems sort of dull and tame.
I mean, top that".

More images upon the screen
More flames
Greed, anger, ignorance
Our nasty little desires
Flames not halted by water
The Buddha smiles
I close my eyes and
Slip into the night—
In this dream no image
Just the idea of solid immensity
The night hidden deep
Within the night
The flowing black water
Of all life's mystery
The black water silently flowing
The clear thin ringing
Of the stars

LOS ANGELES EARTHQUAKE

4:31 A.M. JANUARY 17, 1994

The earth, too, is afraid
I tell you
The earth is afraid
There are far greater earthquakes
In the depths through which
It palpitates
Far deeper black

4:31 a.m.
First the roar
Then out the window I see Venice
Rock in the enormous unseen arms
It looks like the end of the world

I stand in the middle of the room
Now a profound black
All I see are my bare white feet

Beneath them the floor is invisible
Only a blind rage of waves
The language of cataclysm
A crucifixion of winds
It is as if all that exists
Are these black winds
And my bare white feet
Which I am surprised to see
Begin to glow

Glowing, floating above a sea
Of endless night
This cemetery of space
Nightbloom of terrors
Even the breath crumbles
In this tomb of blind eyes
This mirage of deepest black
This terrible hoof of God

As I watch my iridescent feet
The movement stops
Naked, fragile
I reach for my crucifix

Draped only in the large black nun's cross
I, now, a bride
Of the slow, trembling Eternity

The earth, too, is afraid
Naked, fragile
That God is unfathomable
That our shouts
Do not turn the world
That heaven and earth
Shall be smashed in the darkness
And pass away

COLD ELLISON VIII

The mountains come bouncing and roaring into the room.
John Thomas rolls from the bed, sits cross-legged on the floor.
I haven't seen him in this position in awhile. Buddha-like.
Although he says he sits this way always in his mind.
I stand erect in the middle of the room.
Beneath me my bare white feet begin to glow.
My ghostly feet floating over precipices of black,
This plunging night, this
Night within night.

The movement stops. Outside the fire alarm clangs.
Water pours in torrents from the roof. There are shouts,
"Evacuate the building immediately! Cracks in the stairwell."
Later: the water off, fire alarm off. Most cracks are superficial.
Only the top floor is destroyed.

In our room the large hanging Buddhist Temple bell
Is tilted upward as if frozen in the act of ringing.
Behind it, the image of John' Zen master Suzuki Roshi
Now bent forward as in half bow,
As if bowing to the earthquake.

The only object broken is the glass frame
Of our wedding calligraphy by my Zen master Maezumi Roshi
The image which flowed from his brush for us that day—
White plum blossoms falling in the snow."
Now fallen from its ledge high atop the room,
In a full forward bow.

"Now not even glass is between us," John says.
"If I had a thread of attachment to this world," I say,
"This earthquake has severed it."

"What world?" he yawns.

No glass
No falling world
Like plum blossoms in the snow

Below me my naked feet
No longer glow
But above me
The moon rings
The mountains, now taller
Flash their halos

GREAT ZEN FUNERAL

A good day for a
Bukowski funeral
LA's having a
Heat wave
The sky parchment
The starched air
Brittle
In the afternoon light

Here in the chapel
Bukowski's casket is
Wooden, shining
Beside the huge
Red letters
"HANK"

One of the officiating
Buddhist monks has a
Large black
Ink stain
On his saffron robe
Right where he
Sits

Linda Bukowski wears
Her husband's wrist watch
Still ticking
As Sean Penn quotes Hank
"Let's suck the shit out
Of death."

Afterwards, being wheeled
Down the slope
To the gravesite
The casket
Teeters, starts
To roll out of control
The pall bearers

Catch it in time
Then think to let
It go again.
One says, "He's

In there saying,
"Do it! Do it!"
But they do not
At the gravesite
Another monk
Places the last
Red rose
On the casket
Turns, smiles toothily
For the camera

It ends.
People stand around
Not knowing what
To do
"As every ending
Should" John Thomas
Says behind
Me

I walk up to the casket
Stroke it
John follows
Gives it a thump
"He heard that one"
Linda says

At the house
There I talk of
The night before
Hank in the
Mortuary viewing room
Stretched out there
Smiling
In his racetrack outfit
Two pens in his
Breast pocket
Michael Montfort
Had patted
The back of
Hank's writing hand
Said it felt like
Cement
The Mexicans in the
Adjacent viewing room
We're having pizza and Pepsi

Linda moves constantly
Among the guests
John Martin
Carl Weissner
Gerald Locklin
Re, Kim, Concepción
Her stepdaughter Marina
From room to room
Among the cats
Out into the yard
Back again
Checking every corner
"What are you
Looking for, Linda""
"'Hank," she says

Outside on the front steps
I watch the moon
Turn the sky
The poet, his face
Now, the inky night
His voice black wind
Hard mouth, hand
Cut slab of stone
But even in slumber
The ghosts of his poems
Still rising
Alarm
The air

My eyelids become leaden
Linda puts me to bed
She gives me
Hank's pajamas
"The ones he wore
To the hospital."
Freshly laundered.
"This is your home, now"
She tells me.
Her eyes, tiny
Brown suns.
"This is your home."

I drift in and out of
A dreamless sleep in
Bukowski's pajamas
The most comfortable
Pajamas I ever slept in
John sits all night
In Hank's easy chair.
He is saying,
"I can't see how Philomene and Hank
Can stand pajamas!"
Linda is laughing –
Chimes
Great slumber
Great Zen funeral

In my dreamless sleep
The night is the
Round black eyes of
Horses
Just past the
Home stretch
No more need for
Rein or spur or
Snap of the
Whip
All that is heard
Is the faint ringing
Of their long streaming
Manes in the distance
And the dust

See, Hank,
The dust is luminous!

OBSERVATIONS ON THE COLOR BLACK

(Griffith's Observatory July, 1994)
For Wanda Coleman

In the shining
Black wound
Of night
Jupiter
Scarred wind
Blind red eye
And the comet
Flower of what
Broken sun?
Its long-drawn trail
Of frozen petals
Across the
Blazing black
This intimacy
Seed of ice
Spinning womb
Of winds
What immense Black Lover?

PORTRAIT OF MY DAUGHTER

(For her thirtieth birthday)

A reddish brown sky
In her hair
Her eyes
Dark brown winds
Her mouth
Carved by a half moon

My daughter Maureen
Of the sourceless seas

SONNET FOR JOHN THOMAS

Shall I compare you to a winter's night?
You are more tempestuous
Beside you ice is not as quiet
And January young and impetuous
No stormy wind has pitch to match your magnitude
Within your voice all other sounds are lost
One winter's leaf has not your solitude
No single purple rose contains your frost
Within your hush the dripping icicle quakes
And melting snows thunderous in your icy ruins
Below the surface of your frozen lakes
There are more older, colder moons
There is every season of snow, my love, you promise
In the Eternal Winter of John Thomas

POEM FOR MY DAUGHTER

Maureen—
Over
The quiet
Ice
Slick and
Steaming
At her feet
Her
Gestures
Of white
Silence
Her scalding
Calm
Of solitude

BLACK BUDDHA IN A DARK ALLEY

"The jewel of no price which cannot be used up...
Its brilliance illuminates the Universe"
  —Song of Enlightenment, The Zen Master Yoka Genkaku

I had dropped a can of Pepsi
In a Venice alley
The spray of soda shot up
Like the universe exploding
Boiling up into the cold sky

It was then I saw him
Black Buddha in a dark ally
He walked with stone solitude
Nothing held him
Homeless
His young face eroded
An ebony rock
The black night on his tongue
He picked up the Pepsi
And began to drink

"Would you like one that is NOT broken?"
I asked this broken man
(This unbroken man).
My voice was an empty echo
As the night rolled over my eyes

His voice: "Thank you, Ma'am,
Thank you, thank you,"
His stone face smiling
Into the alley resembling a dream
Turned the night sky, gold
And cut the raging rock of the world

HERMITS IN GREATER LOS ANGELES

The City of Angels
Has its hermits

Some take to Disneyland
For their annual retreat
But they never return

One hermit is a
Los Angeles Lakers' basketball cheerleader
I know a Venice hermit who has another hermit
In her refrigerator
In the form of her dead cat

The best kind of hermits are those
That don't know they are hermits
Some have no eyelashes
Scorched from looking too closely

There are those who lose their voices
If they look hard enough they'll find it
In their second pocket of their second suit

Then earthquakes come, jumbling it up again
Like a residential milk shake so that it
Takes an act of faith to believe in sunrise

AN ORDINARY DAY OF WRITING

(When I not writing – John had this dream – which stimulated me to write this poem).

Last night John Thomas dreamed of
A pen that writes
In gold and never lifts
From the paper
Its golden ink
Tarnishes with time
Turns black

Perhaps all poems
Once were gold
And we see them
Finally, in black

Once I dreamed
My writing finger
Was a diamond

Few see them
But often as I write
Purple roses surround
My forehead
They are not dead
Their violet blood has
Simply spilled
Into my pen

As I write
In this room of mirrors
I always wear white
My face becomes
Whiter still

At evening
I listen
To the scraping sounds
Of moonlight
While outside
The sea is glass
Mirrors are hidden
In every stone
The winds have gone
Into sleep, into ice
And I am no longer here

MY SISTER THE PAINTER

(For Pegarty Long)

Hers was
The first cry
That I heard
In my first
Morning
It was she
Who cried
My eyes open

And now she paints, she paints
And where her brush
Touches the canvas
The morning sky
Slams into it
A cry of light

AMERICA: ON THE RAILS

*(Across America quicker than a Zen slap
and not very far behind God.)*

I awaken every morning with
The rhythms of the train
On first opening my eyes, my bed
Appears to be the train the
Southern California morning light through
My window is the brightness of
America passing

As dream time by the Pacific
Dissolves into awakening
Clearly, I am back again in
My room in Los Angeles
It had been the delicate pulsing
Of blood through my veins
Reminding my sleeping mind of
The cadence of the rails

Just returned from journey
To discover America backwards
From the new America of Southern California
To the old America of Boston, Massachusetts
A line through its center from the
Southwest tip of America
Ending at the uppermost East
Atop the great spinning tracks on
Amtrak's South West Chief

Across this land consumed
By luminous skies to the beat of
Clack, clackety clack, clackety
Clackety clack, clackety clack
The trip beginning with the jolt of
The train, more than nudge, less than
A thrust, just enough to remind
Us exactly what we sit upon.
In the language of trains it means
"I am here" not violent, but an
Exquisite power felt rippling
Through spine to brain
One recognizes it from past

Or, feeling it for the first time,
Knows it is different from any
Other touch

Ghostly reader, fellow traveler,
On whichever train you ride;
The glistening rails of America
Or the shinning ghosting tracks
Of your imagination,
Your body understands the language
Of the train, senses the touch, the
Wheels against rails which give
Slightly under the weight of cars
In that moment there is no sound,
Only the feel of it and then
The wheels come up against the spot
Where one rail connects with the next.
There, right there, a faint crack, there at
The joint, right there the beat of that

Crack: clack, clackety-clack,
Clackety-clack, clackety-clack,
The beat of clackety-clackety,
Clack, clack, clackety-clack
And then, the lonesome cry of the whistle
In my ears, the saddest most beautiful of all sounds
As the train begins its gentle rocking
Moving from my city
Into the night, into our amniotic sleep

For to sleep on the train is to sleep
In the womb; its gentle swaying
At times abrupt, as if Mother
Had turned abruptly in her bed
In her own sleep.
And then to awaken to the whistle's
Call over the

America of Arizona—Burning earth. 10,000 years of
Unwritten human history
But the land remembers; has written it
In the ochre mountains
Their faces, cracked by time

America of New Mexico—
Skies as though the wind caught fire
From an incomprehensible solitude

America of Colorado—
Where low cumulus clouds roll
Over endless blue skies of
Ecstasy, grief, and sleep
Towards

America of the Great Plains
Giant green footprint of ice
Green winds, grassy flames
Dotted with drowsy cattle
Through them the train's
Labyrinth of rails

And then, again, the whistle...
At times all the world's sadness
Disappears into the moan of that sound
All its hurt soothed by the train's lulling motion

Through lightning storms of New England
And then to begin the return
From the Boston of America's birth
Through long underground tunnel
But there will be light at its end
So much light...

Upper New York State Satori
As the train winds over a river
The sun sets behind the hills
As the train plummets deep, deep
Into, seemingly, the pupil of the
Sun, the train winding over a
Thin silver river, but it is
As if the river, which weaves
Beneath us, threads us with silvery
Light as if it becomes the train
The train and the river the same
Among the gold splattered leaves, the
Silver speckled waters and the
Sun setting again behind the
Hills, the rising, again, golden
The leaves of trees flecked, mottled

Dotted streaked gold disappearing
Into our eyes, blast of light, all
Encompassing, a few dark trunks
Of trees remaining, then they, too
Gone— only the river's silver
Then it, too gone— disappearing
Into Golden Eternity

It is the only time in the train
That even the babies are silent
There is only the sound
Of her travelers' breaths
In awe of that light rising, falling
As we are, muted by awe
Blinded by awe
Consumed by light
I whisper: "What could express this?
Could a poem ever contain it?"
And at this moment, an old man
In the next seat speaks out loud
"Beautiful," he says
"As it was in the beginning
Is now and ever shall be."

Ah! America!
The name, itself,
Begins with awe
Ends with awe
America!

OH! ALLEN, HOWL FOR US WITH YOUR GHOSTLY TONGUE

Eulogy for Allen Ginsberg

(This poem was begun before his death and I sent it to Allen after he died.)

Allen Ginsberg
Burning shadow
Of Blakean angel
Footprint on
Whitman's grass
Beat of
Kerouac's unchangeable heart
Of Heaven
Allen Ginsberg
Creaking
To Eternity
In William's red wagon

Your voice
Red wind of the moon
Your pen
Candle revealing
The bottom of the sea

Allen Ginsberg
The only author
I happily saw
At the LA Times Book Awards
With holes in his shoes

Oh! Allen
Howl for us
With your ghostly tongue

JACK MICHELINE THROUGH THE EYES OF A DYING COCK ROACH

"The poet is the roach that never gave up!"
—Jack Micheline

(Written for a memorial for Jack Micheline event at Skylight books. As I read it, John Thomas held up Pegarty Long's photos of the reading we had given with Jack Micheline with the dying cock roach and S.A. Griffin saving it.)

"Jack" I said,
"Walt Whitman had nightmares of you"
"Put that in writing," Micheline replied

This was the night
 S.A. Griffin saved the life of a cockroach
From near drowning in a beer bottle
(A momentary triumph of life over death)
So that it could live long enough to hear
Jack Micheline celebrate himself

Beaten with no chaser
At the side of the stage
The insect lay exhausted
Drops of beer in its small vacuoles
Belly up, legs apart, feelers flaccid
In a state of complete receptivity
(The finest way I know to receive poetry)
I suppose it was enchanted –

Micheline's shrieks and gesticulations
The spray of words and spittle
The scattering of crumbs
It appeared as though the poet was being tickled by
Ten thousand cockroach antennae simultaneously

"Stay angry" he shouted
"The world's a put up job
Most people suck
Slave to the boss
No mind of their own
Most people lost souls of the universe
Worry what their neighbor says

Believe in the newspapers
Watch T.V.

Cry in barrooms
Never get enough
Most are scared to death to move their left toe"

Then came a trembling below Jack's belt
And a darkening at the crotch
As he peed in his light beige pants
Long and thin stretched the stain
Like a tiny, but growing Israel
The roach delighted in
Every minute movement
Every subtle scent

"Most people in this world play the game,"
Jack continued,
"Most people never found out who they were
Never had a chance to find out"

I am sure that the now-enlightened roach
Musing on the waving antennae of Micheline's hair
Recalled the line from Whitman:
"The smallest sprout shows
There is really no death."

After the reading
Alone, now, on the stage
The blessed cockroach lay dying
Dying and dreaming it was
A large declaiming poet
In wet pants

EULOGY FOR WILLIAM MARGOLIS

*"Passion does not go without a curse:
only a cursed share is set aside
for that part of human life which has
the greatest significance." —Georges Bataille*

Was William Margolis
The object of a privileged curse?
Was it a form of paralysis
Or extreme lucidity
Or are they not often the same?

Although to be among the Chosen
To be always crossing the desert
Never to arrive at the Promised Land
For over forty years he wandered
Wheeling across the desert of the poem
In its unquenchable thirst
For the blood of the poet

In arid rooms
He collected his own parched relics
Collected each of his petrified mustaches
In small see-through plastic jars
Constructed chests of drawers out of matchboxes
In them pebbles, cracked stamps
Brittle chicken bones, dried-up pen points
In one of the little matchbox drawers
Notes from fortune cookies
Promises of travel, success in some venture
And to take along on his journey to the poem
Artfully wrapped in a tiny gold-foil package
A torn coupon for a 50-cent cup of coffee

Inside a vial there are pencil stubs
All about an inch long
All sharpened to a fine point
And inside that vial, a glass cube
Containing even smaller pencil stubs
Sharpened right down to the metal
Points sharp as cactus needles

On the pencil stubs all erasers were perfect
Perhaps, for him, the poem itself was an eraser

And what was there left to erase?
The dunes of time?
Such a burden of time
Until at last
Time itself became timeless
Time erased time
And then came the poem's demand
That he erase himself

Once in the Venice Temple
I shouted into the crowded room
"WHAT IS THE POEM?"
William Margolis replied
"The poem is black on black."

Yes, Will
In the end the poem is written
Not to be heard but to be burned
It is to be always blindly crossing
Never arriving
Its desert road black on black
Until (as it is with you, now, Will)
In the hot winds of the poem
The blood of the poet hardens
Into cactus, into grit
Then, finally, like a leisurely joke
The cactus flowers bloom
And the sands become fire

EULOGY FOR SHIRLEY CLARKE

Shirley,
Your camera
Like a needle in broken rooms
Pricks the men and women
With knee caps of carpet

The camera can not save them
Nor you, with no saving church bell
Yet behind your lens
A billion suns burning
On that needle tip
Your images traveling
From the spark of light
The drug vein seething, opening
Marking the blood of time
Moving in a cloud of cinema vapor
In an acetate theater
Like big Black aging jazz man
Blowing in his sad ecstasy

All the while you move
In a cool world
With no false steps
No indecision at all
Carrying it all out to the limits
To bleed the eye
To bleed the "I"

Shirley,
You played all the parts well
Stately, elegant movements
A captive, tortured by your own talents
Even if it comes to nothing in the end
Your films —
Black and white ruins blazing
Move into time with the music
Like saxophone
Like blood speaking
In the silence

IN PEGARTY'S BURGUNDY ROOM

Cracked glass mirrors
Cast rainbows
Her eyes
Green windows

In the golden night
Remembering a sunset
She looks to
A far away moon

Velvet curtains sway
With the slightest breeze
Before the slow California sky

High on her wall
A portrait she has painted
Of a small red doll
It has her own smile
Her paintings have
The simplest line
Even the joyous shoelace

Lately I have come to this room
To sit in her wine velvet chair
I come to tell her
"I find it dangerous to be a poet
I will soon to be sprawled in vacant lots
In every gutter of this town
I wish to be as far from my body as possible"

Cracking, my voice spills
Into her mirrors
Her palms open
Like narrow paths
The mountains are not far away

Her open palms
The comfort of this room
Do not come into the world's eyes
To the crowd beneath her window
Roaring with confidence and greed

There have been others
And there will be more
But none like she

ROGER PENNEY,
DEATH CANNOT CLOSE YOUR EYES

(November 19, 1939 – January 6, 1998 4:30 p.m.)

"So that an afternoon becomes all existence, or better: all existence is like one long afternoon"— *Vicente Aleixandre*

It is half-past-four in the afternoon
Your fall the sound of
Thunder in the distance
Your corpse alone, naked
Your eyes blue translucent, half closed
Your eyes now full of every sky
Your eyes blue jacaranda blossoms

At half-past-four in the afternoon
Alone I watch the blue line
That divides sky from sea
Somehow I go where you are going

Ours is a long afternoon that lasts a lifetime
Like an afternoon in a room
Full of love and jacaranda blossoms
Where all the light in the universe suddenly gathers
"Lightning comes from the ground up" you say
"The suddenness of your green eyes" you say
In an afternoon of half closed eyes

At half-past-four in the afternoon
It is as if we are lying down again
The same afternoon lovers
Lying uncovered, glowing bodies
In a room beneath a jacaranda tree
"I want to be in your eyes" you say
"It is always your eyes that destroy time" you say

In an endless afternoon
I am inside your eyes
Your life now gone like an afternoon
Far away, you are closer still
I touch the delicate warm edges
Of your hushed body, its widening boundaries
Now, no longer wounded by our fire

It is half-past-four in a darkening world
The thick light buries us
In another nakedness
And in this poem
Only your eyes
Roger Penney –
Death cannot close your eyes

THE PAINTINGS, SOMEHOW, MUST HAVE FELT IT

(For Roger Penney)

I watch from inside a portrait you painted of me
which hangs on your wall along the staircase
as you climb for the last time, your heart in its final beats
its pulse so often I've felt press fast, faster against my chest
while you say, "I want to die over and over again in your eyes"
as I pronounce your name… as I pronounce it now, Roger
I think of you climbing those stairs
each heart beat one less, one less, one less
I am with you in every brush stroke of that painting
as you ascend, as the death comes
I watch in your final need comes— so intense
all the portraits you painted of me must, somehow, feel it
and I know you will say those words as you fall
"to die in your eyes, over and over, to die in your eyes"
and you will hear me pronounce your name, Roger
and even now you come to me, Roger, Roger
come to me… come to me…

POEMS ARE THE WORLD ASLEEP

Poems are
The world asleep
Where death
Cannot reside

DROPPED UNDER THE SKIN OF LIFE

"And you adopt, lost, when something broke And let you from a dream."
—*Emily Dickinson*

Under the skin of life:
The thrustling and jostling
Ideas, like immortal stains

They snore in stuffy, ugly rooms
Without a dream
Some infallible doctrine
One cannot stomach
Some convinced experienced desire
That sort of blind knowledge

The very structure of thought
(Which I am, now, trying in vain
To bring to its knees)
Is catastrophic

God has no opinions

The intimate springs of life
Are choked by a splendid thought,
A self-engendered
 ecstasy

The real world
Is a crucifix
In a pale mother's hand

POEM FOR MY FATHER

His eyes show me things
So small
As to be large
Beyond measure

And now the glistening eye is closed
Now, to his child
Nothing is understood
Without the geography
Of his eye
That he not see, not speak
That the countries of his mind
Should sleep —
Hardly a reality

Now, the world is not enough
The sky, the sea
For it is he who saved it
Again and again
By seeing it

And when he sleeps
The world sleeps
But not as well

CRUSHED PIGEON WITH THE SECRET

Crushed pigeon
On the pavement
No head
No breast
A mere gray smudge
With only one wing erect
Moving gently in the
Afternoon breeze

All life fluttered
In that wing
Gray feathers splayed
It flew-
Higher, wider
A wing to cover
All Jerusalem

"O Jerusalem, Jerusalem,"
(I sing Isaiah's lamentation to the dead bird)
"How often would I have gathered
Thy children together even as a hen
Gathered her chicks under her wing
And you would not...

As one whose mother's comforts,
So will I comfort you;
And you will be comforted in Jerusalem."

Gray cement. Gray pigeon:
Life and death at once
A wing, a tongue
About to call to utter,
Bringing to my page:
The great secret
The word, the world itself

At this very moment
John walks in the door
A door slammed behind me in the room
Slammed shut – the door to the poem.
The wing had been writing itself
As though flying
Only once

Only once
Could not hear it again
Gone
Left
No more than what was already known
An impeccable symmetry – life, death

No word
Only that image –
Smashed gray carcass
On a gray road
Above it the gray wing
Swaying in the breeze

But no crushing wheel
Can take away
This Secret—
Winged, fluttering,
Unutterable, but perishable
Perfect

A MONSTROUS ROOT

Night
Climbs
The purple grasses
It cannot be buried
The raven knows
The darkness
Is a monstrous root

THE HUNGER

The poem
Is composed largely
Of the hunger
To write it

Great dirty hand-print
In the sky

MARRIAGE VOWS

We open a door
To where
There is no road

We take it

I WRITE AS THE MUSE REQUIRES

I step inside the poem.
I can barely see in the mirror
Which is her sky

Through its cracks
(Let me say this carefully)
I see her poets—
Their diamond eyes
Their lips of black velvet

But they are not enough to save
The world from falling, falling
Nevertheless
She exacts yet another death

Naked, they lie face down
Before a greater silence
A greater blackness
I cry out to them
But they do not hear my wailing
Nor do I

I speak to myself with an
Alphabet that flows
Thick like blood
At the edge of darkness

I no longer know
What I have lost
Then finally—
The poem's agony of light

MIRRORS ARE SLEEPING WINDS

Mirrors are
Sleeping winds

In this glass room
Its window
Dreams into frost

Hours after hours pass

I sit before it
Death
Swinging in slowly
In her pleated black skirt

The night, black
As patent leather shoes

It is palatable, the sounds
Of the newly dead
Grinding their teeth
In a grin of relief
Too soon to be ghosts
Too late to speak

As I, neither fully dead
Nor fully alive
Sit with them
Upon their marble lakes

I do not feel
Their marble kisses

Upon the poems
Steaming on
My marble lips

THE POEM A SCALPEL

To slice
The voice open
To reveal the allure
The roaring hills
Through which
Tallest miracles
Stalk

Its luminosity
Slashes

LAST CONFESSION

My life has been
A terrified eye
Dedicated to ruin
Perhaps another winter
Will level me to dust
Put me in the mud

There will come a time
When my opinions
Will have vanished
Into thunder
Afterwards
(Again!)
I'll plunge headlong
Into sleep
And dream
That I am struck by lightning

I confess
I observed carelessly
And turned away too soon
I took my everyday excuses
From the common stock
My timidity was a
Weakness quickly seen and
Exploited by the world
As was my arrogance
Finally, I came to regret
Having bent the blades of grass
Beneath my feet

There were moments
When my mind scarcely
Belonged to me at all
Imprisoned
In the bizarre shapes of matter

Inward was the only direction
Not closed to me
A luminous point
To which the eye loves to return
To detach myself for hours
From my species

Still, I managed
To live and die
Deep over my head
In an ocean of light

Some of my poems
Are its silence uttered
Truth is utter silence

THE GHOSTS OF VENICE WEST

They are already ghosts
John and Philomene
As they pass
Along the Boardwalk
This highway of poetry and death
Where ghosts and poets overlap
As they pass, the gulls
Ghosting above their shadows

Everything's haunting everything

Already ghosts
John and Philomene
Under the ghosts lamp posts
Of Venice West
Their cadence
The breath of sleep
At rest
Lost at the edge of America
Already ghosts
And each poem
Already a farewell

Everything's haunting everything
The sea is the ghost of the world

POEM TO AN UNBORN

(For my Grandson)

Curled
Sleeping
In the towering dark

In the womb
Shadowy fold
Of eternity

Your first breath
Not yet taken

For one more moon
(The world averted)
You do not see us
Nor we, you

But already
You are loved

The Raven Poems

NINE WAYS OF LOOKING AT A RAVEN

(For Aya)

One can never see a raven
Without hearing a poem

Like the poem
The raven can fly upside-down
And gives no reply to questions

In the raven's eye:
A spot which
Disappears in the distance

A mirror is the eyes
Of a thousand ravens

The raven, even with other ravens
Is always by itself

The raven is the friend
In the room of the dead

The raven has
Tucked beneath its wings
The whole world

At dawn the raven is
A red door

Night is the dream
Of the first raven

CRY OF THE RAVENS

(For Ian Conner)

In every raven's beak
Waits the high note
Maria Callas sings in Tosca

Beethoven's 5th Symphony is the
Black and beating iridescent breast
Of a raven

Once they crucified a raven
Michelangelo delivered it
From marble
Gently placed it
Against that breast
The Pieta

Van Gogh's last brush stroke
Was a raven's wing

Isadora on her talons
Sprang into flight

Poe was, is
His Raven

The first raven
The white raven
Emily Dickinson

Every raven
On its night perch
Is a Zen master

A raven spins, sleeping
In the womb of the world

The blinding light in the tomb
Is the raven

Listen
The cry of ravens
Tilting the wind
Turning the world
Throats full
Of the first word
Every word
All poems
Not yet written

Listen
The distant cry
Grows louder

In the black luster
Of sleep
The world becomes
Untangled
Echoing
The cry of ravens

THERE ARE NEVER ENOUGH RAVENS IN A POEM

(For Pegarty)

The moon
If it could
Would be a
Raven

Many stars
Strive to be Ravens

Lightning is the slow
Raven

Most Ravens have been seduced
By the blind

The Mother of us all is
The uncarved Raven

I write, always
With a Raven's quill
Between my fingers

There are never enough
Ravens in a poem

A Book of Hours

THE ANNUNCIATION

Proud, sullen world
The great hour
Comes closer
The latch about
To be lifted
The door about to open
This hour of light and dust
In Nazareth

Gabrielle steps
Across the threshold, says
"Fear not, Mary."
But it is the angel who is afraid
Of her silence,
The rush into her womb.

Then, the trembling.
Gabrielle can no longer look
Upon her flushed face,
Leaves her
In the world's most
Solitary hour
When only she knows

This smallest tremor
Alone in her water
In her womb
God's golden seed of humility.

NATIVITY

Gentle Lightning
Impossible white hush of winter
The complete forgiveness of snow
Golden blade of sunrise
Burning grape
Seed of wheat and wind
Incurable wound of compassion
A blossom, poor as the moon

And then the small revelation
Is forgotten, but AH!
The sleeping arrow
The love that flashed
Through the air!

THE CRUCIFIXION

This crime of Heaven
This fury of compassion
Beneath a crown
Of wind and whips
Bleeding eyes
Bleeding beard
His beautiful body
On the crossed tree
Rising, falling
His blood glistening
In the noon sun

The coppery taste of blood
In his mouth
He is calling
Death slick on his tongue
He is calling
"Eloi! Eloi! Lama Sabacthani!"
Nothing else is heard
But the immense weeping

It is three in the afternoon
And He sees His huge shadow
Over the mob
Its stretch of agony
Across Jerusalem
All names drown
In His blood
Nailed, naked, caught
Between Heaven and earth
This King of Grief
This lamentation
In the sky-
A hurricane
Of silences

EASTER

Now death is in collision
With life

His ripped palms and feet
Luminous
His teeth of fire
Smiling through the tomb

Neither flesh nor spirit

This descent of love
This sudden spark
Which leaped

This day
It is the world
Guttering like a dying candle
Is now transparent
All smoke and
Smoldering dreams.

PENTECOST

Our flesh, now
A dazzling sepulcher
The fire that strikes
Must burn
Must burn

2000s

POEM FOR MY SON

As a young boy
My son Patrick
Saved the lives
Of neighborhood
Insects
Once I saw him
Press on
A drowning beetles'
Abdomen
A bubble popped out
Of its tiny mouth
It lived

And always, with him
There were the frogs
Each would gaze
At the other
Silently
And for a long time
Then the boy
Would extend
His gentle hand
And the frog
Leap lightly
Into his open palm

Patrick would exclaim:
"We love crickets
So there are crickets!"

Patrick cried:
"You just stepped on the best
Worm I ever had!"

Patrick sang:
"I feel like a hippopotamus
On a diet
 In the spring."

Patrick philosophized:
"If you wake up
And don't touch anything
It won't be a real day."

The pounding machinery
Of religious ideas
Deafens me
It was from rugged mountains
And still waters
That the Zen ancestors first emerged
It is there I would return
And to my son, Patrick
Whose lightness of being
Outweighs theology

PINK CLOUD POEM

I walk out on the beach —-
 only one pink cloud
and it above my head –
low in the sky.
Such silence!
I raise my writing book
as if it is a chalice
and pen
for the cloud to give me
a poem
A soft rain fell.
The poem fell
onto the page –
 Such silence!

—August 31, 2000

WEDDING POEM

On your behalf, Valarie and Kent,
We have invoked Mnemosyne, Memory,
Mother of all the Muses.
She will come to you now, enter you,
and you will remember
This glorious second day of June
together and forever.

—Philomene Long & John Thomas

ROMANCE AMONG THE MORNING GLORIES
(HIGH BUT SUBTLE)

Each morning I detach them
But soon they are at it again
Reaching for each other
Clinging

When I hold a young one
Called "Heavenly Blue"
It clasps my finger like a newborn

There is much slow
But persistent growing
Going on around this lively world
Like the grandson in my daughter's womb

QUESTIONS

The world, is it called the "rolling void"?
And what makes a nun
Different from other women?
Why do they continue to try
Under seemingly insurmountable obstacles?

Is it true –
That one out of every species of mammal
Is a bat?
Are there words in the wind?
If so, do the eucalyptus create them?

It is true
How poor we are
Little more than naked
That the last thing removed is
A worn gold watch, a worn ruby ring
Then, naked to the crematorium.

Is it true?
The dead in L.A.
(Except during earthquakes)
Rarely change positions

And those slopes of sorrow
Are there grimaces or smiles beneath the earth?
Ink stains still on fingertips?
My late husband, I am told,
Wrote several revisions of
His suicide note

My dead baby, Carhirmee
A splinter now
She, who lived one day
Is it true?
That it is, as I've been told,
Better to live one day
Than not at all?

ADAM

This is the Garden, Adam, and
You've just eaten the Apple.
No Cain or Abel yet,
Just little Aidan.

No going back, now, Dad —
And to us you are
The first Father.

— Philomene & John, Father's Day, 2001

AIDAN

"Little fire"
Sets off all our fire detectors
Even the firemen with their hoses
Couldn't put you out
Where is the extinguisher
When we need it?
Hold still!
We're trying to toast
These marshmallows!

— Gran' Philomene & Gran' John

MAUREEN

All dream — and whose?
Fire burning far out at sea

Maureen holds Aidan
The Great Water nourishes
The tiny flame. No dream.

— John & Philomene, Mother's Day 2001

IN THE PRIVACY OF MIRRORS

(I believe first poem written when John was gone.)

In the privacy of mirrors
The face comes loose
Impossible
No one here
The no one
That tends sleep

PEGARTY PEGARTY PEGARTY

There, the wheels to rail a softer sound a softer pitch
like clarity clarity
sounds like pegarty pegarty
on the road to Queen Mary
with running from the Italians
Pegarty, Pegarty, Pegarty....
Whose might and innocence
Makes make me weep

THE PACIFIC

Burning blue bell of time
Before the great unmade bed—
Los Angeles
Its sleepers gurgling
In another sea
Awake to yet another sleep
Each wave
An underwater chime
From its great depth
Its absence
Left by the moon
Its absence
Filled by the sky

THE SEA

The sea— a forever startling
Temple of time

Radiance undisturbed

Delicate press
Stubborn flesh!

FRAGMENTS

Time is not an abstraction
Some day dust
Will replace the sea

*

The carcasses of imagery
I tell myself I am not one of them

*

Maltreatment of a house fly

*

The still point from when and where
We began
Is right here
This very point which drives the pen

*

Poems are living ruins

*

Memory is debris

*

Shadows are a slow hysteria

*

Los Angeles: City over cracked stone.

POEM TO LOST POEMS

I have fondness for them
whatever state they are in now

possibly – just about to become words again
but just that they once
that they were once

But where are they now?
They same place as the poems not yet written
or never to be written?

One caught behind a small hair in my nostril
Moving back and forth, back and forth
with each breath — winds fraying it like
a Tibetan prayer flag?

And all those poems that for five years I secretly dropped
Into nun's pockets?
Deep black nun's pockets – while they were not looking
Where are they —
Can there be anything so deep and black
as in nun's pockets — and even when they disappear
I'm sure they simply widen
widen as they say night widens —
Once a nun thirty – five years later
came to Venice and said to me:
"Philomene, thank you for the poems."

I love this phrase:
the "architecture of sleep"
(Perhaps that is what poems ARE
the "Architecture of sleep")

if a poem falls alone
in a sleep without a dream
is there a sound?

But all poems inevitably
will be lost
They lie on a bridge
which collapses behind us
But so beautiful
so subtle
The link—
both and neither and between
flesh and God

I AM NOT OF THIS WORLD

I am not of this world
I simply have no more use of it —
Now, only,
 a pail filled with sorrow

A gust of wind
Caught
In the windowpane

Caught deep
Within the earth
The sky
From a lie find a truth

2002

COLD ELLISON IX

(To someone brought up on the Latin Mass, the very name "Cold Ellison" suggests the repeated phrase "Kyrie Eleison"— "Lord, have mercy on us." It is as if Long has moved from "Kyrie Eleison" to "Cold Ellison." — Jack Foley)

Winter, 2002
I walk out to the sunset sea
Walk through a flock of
Sand-roosting sea gulls
Softly, so as not to disturb them
I say, "Allo! Allo!"
Just the way two-year-old
Aidan Sandman-Long does it:
"Allo! Allo!"
Must mean something in seagull
The gulls stare as I say it
Some even follow me
Never losing eye contact

I stand in the middle of the flock
Together, we face the sea
Some are behind me, some in front
I just want to get the feeling of
What it is to be a seagull
Waiting for their sun to set

It is like being a nun in chapel
The backs of their heads looking similar
An occasional jerk of the head
Little movement. But definitely more than
A nun at evening meditation

I suppose for them the sea is an altar
And the golden-orange disk of the sun
Their glowing Eucharist
Perhaps my "Allo!" is their "Alleluia!"
Because they love it when I say
"Allo! Allo!"
They never seem to tire of my
"Allo! Allo!"

—February 23, 2002

19TH ANNIVERSARY POEM

*(The following poems were written after John passed away.
March 29, 2002 19th 3:00 PM.
Anniversary was written the week after for his memorial.)*

"Should you desire the Great Tranquility be prepared to sweat white beads."
— *Zen Master Hakuin*

You sit, my love, a crumpled man in a hospital wheel chair:
Belly swollen, leg swollen, red; hands pale, thin.
(Hands I have so often felt cupped over the crown of my head.)
I tell you that I am writing our anniversary poem.
You smile. I tell you it is a fine one,
That it is deep in my heart as I speak.
You tell me that you, too, have an anniversary poem
Not yet on paper. But, also, a fine one.
It comes from a dream you had of Heaven:
There is a Heaven coexisting alongside us,
Even interpenetrating,
And that you and I can step into it in many strange ways:
Through pigeons, seeds, the final hand clap,
  Through abandoned garbage,
  By an out-of-business coffee shop in Death Valley.

You do not know that you will never finish the poem.

Of our love, our life, you say:
"If I die, it can't touch it.
If you die, it can't touch it.
If we both die, it can't touch it.
Nothing can touch it."

An attendant comes in with another wheelchair,
Because the one in which you sit has no foot rests.
Reaching up to the door posts—-
You begin to rise. Hands trembling —
You are a biblical Samson, shaking Temple columns.
 Legs apart for balance— rising higher
You look like a nine-story statue of Colossus:
Thighs: eleven feet in breath;
Ankles: five feet in diameter.
It is as if I could barely wrap my arms around
One of your fingers.
Then, legs straightened, you stretch so high

It is as though your head will rent the ceiling.
You become Afghanistan's stone Buddha,
The moment before it is shot down into pebbles.
In the dim light you are the color gold —
The risen John Thomas.

Suddenly, you collapse into the next chair under your own weight.
Broken asunder; your fractured ankles, so weak you must ask
An attendant to lift them a mere three inches onto the footrests.

You look at me, place your palm upon your weak heart and
Mouth the words: "My Only One"
You don't have to say it aloud. You and I already know.
For nineteen years we have said it to each other:
Since we first made love on that Good Friday.
(On Easter Sunday when I asked, "How are you?"
Your reply had been: "Resurrected!")

"My Only One."
You say it twice this time.
I place my hand upon my heart and move my lips:
"My Only One. My Only One."
You do not know, but somehow I do:
These are the last words we will say to each other.

We sit still in the silence which
These three words have always created.
But other words enter my mind:
"He is dying"

I watch as someone rolls you away.
Then you are stopped for a moment,
Before leaving through the door.
I watch you look up gratefully at the attendant;
A humble Colossus.

O, Love, Love,
How will I bear it?

I think: This could be my last image of you.
But I will not wave.
I do not want my hand to catch your attention.
You are too weak to turn, to respond.
I know that you would thank me for this small kindness.

I walk down the hall,
Alone, with our unwritten anniversary poems,
This time, saying aloud through the empty hall:
"He is dying. He is dying.

Good Friday.
You went so quickly, the nurse told me.
"He was wearing his oxygen mask;
smiling, waving."
It is a great sorrow of my life that I was not with you.
But I know you would like me to think that
You were waving back at me.
And so I will, Love.
And you are Immense and Golden.

—April 6, 2002

PIETA AT HOLY CROSS CEMETERY

(Meditation upon a replica of Michelangelo's sculpture in the Mausoleum of the Resurrection.)

The marble corpus dangles
Precariously over the Mother's lap
Her right hand alone supports him
Fingers splayed, deep into his rib cage
Her knees apart
As one would balance an infant
Above him, her soft breasts
Seemingly turn marble into flesh

His hair thick with blood
Blood into stone
Lips parted in death
Hers pressed gently in speechless grief

The folds of her dress
Run through his fingers
It is almost as if he reaches for her
From his now mute anguish

Her back is straight, head slightly bent
A thin line across her forehead
In her face, a grieving so severe
It becomes serenity

Her left upturned palm
Opened to receive the world's sorrow
Is at once: a question and acceptance

I reach up
Place my tear-soaked tissue in that hand
In my mind I would climb into the lap
But no, not for me
Not that comfort yet
Must first become
That hand
That face
Become
Rock of sorrow
Eternity in granite
Time and agony
In stone

—September 24, 2002

PIETA IN A LOS ANGELES MORTUARY

"Now, like the gods, he is invulnerable.
Nothing on earth can hurt him."— Borges

John Thomas: stretched upon a gurney
A thin plate of steel; thin steel legs supporting him
At times his enormous body appears suspended in air
It seems to me as if he lies upon a make-shift altar

He had said to me: "This is happening because of our love"
And again, in my mind's ear, I hear the mocking; the laughter
"Look! He doesn't even know how to work his wheel chair!'
"Look at that belly. Is HE pregnant!"

Again I hear him say: "Forgive them. Forgive them all."

Before his pale corpse I cry aloud:
"THEY CRUCIFIED YOU!"
Then place my hand upon his chest, whisper:
"I'm here, Love. I'm here.
You died. You died on Good Friday
On the third hour; the very hour nineteen years ago
When we made love for the first time
I have written our Anniversary poem
And in it I say the: 'Risen John Thomas'
The last words of the poem are: 'Immense' and 'Golden.' "
"And, Love, because that Easter nineteen years ago
When I asked how you were, and you said 'Resurrected!'
I have found you a tomb (It is our tomb)
In a Mausoleum called the 'Sanctuary of the Resurrection'
For there are many resurrections
And this is OUR resurrection."

As I say these words – from his body
A soft golden light rising, finally, encompassing me
It is both passion and oblivion as the world falls away
The room becomes a mirror of suns
And we — as if exploding
Into the "Eye of God"

— April 5, 2002

AT THE CEMETERY, JUNE 2002

(Written after husband John Thomas's death 3:00 p.m., March 29th, 2002)

At cemetery
Widowers, mostly –
(An occasional widow)
On knees, tending to graves
which need no tending.
What do they find to do?

The widow to my left
Trims each blade of grass
Along side a gravestone
On a freshly cut lawn.

It is always the same posture
Within a similar framework —
The cemetery's expanse of green
In the distance a gray, bent silhouette
Silhouette because the mourners
Appear to lose their individuality –
The mourning, itself, a persona

How many widowers, widows
At this moment around the world –
Bent?

— June, 2002

SHE'S A MS. PRUFROCK

She's a Ms. Prufrock
Held together with unease.
Consider her speech as vapor

Charles Olson said:
"Teacher and poet
Are a connected vocation."

One takes a risk in
Reading a poem
It is a maze of wind
Time contained
Only by its length
Begins a world
Ends a world
Yes, entering it
You take a risk
This poem
Any poem

— June 2002

THE POEM TRANSFERS ITS FORCE TO THE READER

The poem transfers its force to the reader
If we really know poetry
Then we must know all its dangers.

— June 22, 2002

JOHN AND I: OUR OWN COUNTRY NOW, ETERNAL PRESENT

(July, 2002. Begin to hear John.)

"She adjusts a chair for a ghost."
None of us are young
And even one of us is dead.
Now only one not young
And two dead.

BECAUSE DEATH, YOU ARE SO SUCCESSFUL I'LL LET YOU WRITE THIS POEM

Madam, Sir
Whichever you prefer.
Take up this pen
Try writing a poem
A word
Anything...

Ah ha! I thought as much
Nothing could come from
A face so smug.

— September , 2002

MARCUS AURELIUS AT A DODGER GAME; KIRK GIBSON UP TO BAT

Dodger Stadium, 1988 World Series
Los Angeles Dodgers & Oakland Athletics
The score: Athletics lead 4 to 3
One man on base
Bottom of the ninth
Outfielder, pinch – hitter, Kirk Gibson is up to bat

I whisper to Marcus Aurelius —
The second century Roman Emperor
Who is sitting next to me:

"Did you notice, Marcus,
The sky seems larger at a baseball game
And the ball is like a small spinning sphere
A miniature sun-bleached earth
Its continents held together with red thread
And how curious— the purpose is to hit it
And then return to home plate –
To go to a lot of trouble
To arrive at where you were in the first place.

The philosopher listens attentively
With his serene, noble face
I understand why he has been called by some
The purest among the human race

Kirk Gibson hobbles up to home plate
His left leg so sore. The day before
He could not so much as jog in place
Nor swing against the air
I explain to Marcus what Gibson hopes to attain

Marcus leans towards me, whispers:
"The pursuit of the unattainable is insanity."
I, too, lean forward, say: "I agree.
I agree with about everything you say –
Why, I often go to sleep with your
Mediations by my bed, but Marcus,
Could we make an exception in baseball?'

I tell him more about Kirk Gibson
"Once someone said that, with his scrubby beard
He was a disgrace to the uniform –
And there was a time the crowd would shout:
"Gibson stinks!'
Marcus replies:
"If you are distressed by anything external,
The pain is not due to the thing itself
But to your own estimate of it.
And this you have power to revoke at any moment."

Ah! Right you are, Marcus! And I know Gibson will do exactly that!

And then the pitch.
Ball one
Strike one
Ball two
Ball three
Strike two

Three balls. Two strikes.

Marcus becomes completely still
As if speaking to Gibson alone:
"Remember your higher Self becomes invincible
when once it withdraws into itself."

Gibson steps off the plate.
Returns.
Eyes the pitcher, thinks:
"Partner, as sure as I'm standing here you're gonna' throw a back-door slider.

In comes a back door slider.

Gibson Swings. CRACK!!
Home run!

If that ball has an inner life
It well might be feeling that it had
Received the original crack

And the crowd cheers as if they, indeed
Are witnessing the beginning of the Universe.

Gibson hobbles 'round the bases
Pumping the sky at his waist
At home base, surrounded by Dodger teammates
He raises his fist high into the night sky

As we leave Dodger Stadium I say,
 "Marcus, did you notice how heroic rhymes with stoic?'

Marcus Aurelius is quiet
His eyes seem rounder, softer.

"That was baseball history, Marcus!!
We just witnessed baseball history, Marcus!"

"Even to those whose lives were a
Blaze of glory," he says, "this comes to pass—
The breath is hardly out of them before,
In Homer's words, they are 'lost to sight alike and hearsay.' "

We are caught in the flow of the departing crowd
Marcus continues:
"What, after all, is immortal fame? An empty, hollow thing.
To what, then, must we aspire? This, and this alone:
The just thought, the unselfish act,
The tongue that utters no falsehood,
The temper that greets each passing event
As something predestined, expected,
An emanating from the One source and origin."

"But, Marcus" I ask, "Do you still believe
That to pursue the unattainable is insanity –
It's fine, isn't it, just once in a while –
to pursue the unattainable
In BASEBALL?"

Marcus does not answer
The current of the crowd pulls him away from me
Soon all I see is the helm of his robe
Swaying with his graceful gait

It too, finally, disappears into the crowd
But far away, above a blur of humanity
I see his right hand rising in a fist; high
Into the immense Los Angeles sky
And in the distance I hear him shout:

"WAY TO GO, KIRK GIBSON!"

September 29, 2002

INGREDIENTS OF GRIEF

Wedged
Between
Life / death
Terror
Is a last veil
Then –
Lost / tossed
By sorrow
(OUT Among the
"Ones Gone
To Bliss" OUT)
And your now
Transparent
Countenance

— November, 2002

FOUND POEM

Our life
This poem
A shadow of lightning

You do not have to speak it
I know

Love,
Daily, nightly
You come
In a mist of silence
From a gaping dream
Our love—
A vulnerable alchemy
Imploding time

— October, 2002

A SWAN IN THE CEMETERY'S POND

A swan
In the cemetery's pond
A half moon
The Muse

— October, 2002

WHERE ELSE DO WALLS GLOW LIKE THIS?

Inside the California Mission of Santa Barbara
Where else do walls glow like this?
Waves of color
As if inside color
As if color was alive.

— October, 2002

INSIDE THIS BLEEDING LYRIC

Inside this bleeding lyric
Our love repeating over. Over
As a sacrament in the poem

An orgasm of pain
And now can hardly hold the pen

I mourn the passing of his body
His mind – but to mourn all
Gone is to deny the mystery
Far deeper, wider....
"The one wealth
The one vast pulsing mystery
At the heart of everything—
This love between us."

Another kind of resurrection
Through poetry – in between
Spirit and matter
Where we
Join

Prose
2002-2006

HOW TO GET ALONG WITH YOUR MOTHER, FATHER, SISTER, BROTHER, EVERY LAST ONE OF YOUR CHILDREN, YOUR GRANDMOTHER, GRANDFATHER, GRANDSON AND GRANDDAUGHTER

Imagine your father is Goliath, your brother is David and they're always going at each other. Your mother Judith has been known (metaphorically) to sever at least one head. The good part is your sister is Ruth, but she'll also tell you that your people are not her people, and she'll be leaving soon. You're all stuffed into Noah's Ark and every one stinks. But allow yourself to be comforted by this thought: Your father could have been Jason (you may remember—he ate his children) and your mother Medea (she served them to him). Even for the gods it can be hell. Imagine you are a Prometheus or a Philomel.

Do not, I repeat, do not amuse yourself with the idea things would be better if you had a father and mother called St. Joseph and St. Mary because that can mean nothing but trouble, beginning with the envy of Your sisters and brothers as You enter a room with all those miracles that You cannot stop from happening.

This is the fact and the friction. It's been happening for 5,000 years of recorded history. It is the human story— the story of every one you see on a sunny Sunday afternoon on the Venice Boardwalk at the corner of Paloma Avenue and Speedway: long-haired Moseses; tattooed Cains and Abels; at least one Judas and many Mary Magdalenes. And recalling Greek theater – in the Venice theatre – there is no shortage of fools; fools in the finest sense of Greek drama.

This is the human family.

It is what makes the Buddhas smile.

Accept it.

Now I may be exaggerating slightly but this has been my experience— at one point you might have children and for the next two decades you are Job on a dung heap: sometimes happily; sometimes not. But you will find you are repeating as you change at least one diaper: "Someone did this for me. Someone did this for me" and someone did this for everyone walking down that Venice Boardwalk on a Sunday afternoon."

It's just as simple as that.

Read your history.

Finally, when your little ones are gone you become Rachel, weeping for her children. Again you will say: "Someone did this for me. Someone cried when I left home."

This brings me to your grandparents.

If you are like me or Adam or Eve, you never saw them (mine were in Ireland) so I know with authority, everyone should be happy to see at least one grandmother or grandfather. And as for your grandchildren the advice is so easy it hardly counts as information. If you have a little fire of a grandson or are expecting a shinning new granddaughter who will wake you up at 2:00 AM, crying and seeming to be as wet as the Pacific Ocean, my suggestion is a simple one. Love them. Love them

—July 2, 2003

SOCRATES AT THE WHITE HOUSE

President George Bush and First Lady Laura Bush
Welcome us with their deep-in-the-heart-of Texas smiles
Socrates says: "The unexamined life is not worth living"
And we all sit down

"Hi Folks!"
President Bush pats the ancient Greek philosopher
On the knee," says, "Now you won't be goin' 'round
corrupting the youth for us, will you?"

Socrates replies:
"If the youth seem to care about riches,
or anything more than about VIRTUE;
I would reprove them,
as I would reprove YOU."

Socrates can be overbearing
Even if he is unassuming:
The large body, white beard;
massive skull which appears an even greater expanse
because there is no hair on the top of it;
Deep, deep set eyes
Behind that mighty oak tree of a nose
If Socrates did not always wear that humble ratty tunic
I think few could remain in a room with him.

He says:
"There are many who think that they know something,
But really know little or nothing. Know yourself."

I say: "And speaking of knowing yourself
Mr. President, did you know that
an inadvertent smile traverses
your lips when you say the word "WAR?"
It is subtle, almost imperceptible
originating from left corner of your mouth."

Laura Bush continues with her three inch deep smile:
"You know, I hadn't noticed that.
I'll look for it next time."

A line forms across the president's brow
His eyebrows begin to take on a life of their own
They look like confused caterpillars

I continue:
"Mr. President, remember
When your father was the president
How he would say: 'Read my lips.'
Well I took his suggestion seriously
That's why I've been watching YOUR lips.
Especially when you pronounce that word WAR
It is my opinion that at that moment you are enjoying it
And your lips are also saying:
LOOK AT ME, DAD! I'M THE PRESIDENT!"

"Now Socrates has a few questions.
He's been listening to your speeches.
And you know him–
He likes to question certainties."

Socrates:
"What do you mean by honor, virtue, morality,
patriotism, freedom . What do you mean by these abstract words
with which you so easily settle the problems of life and death?

Laura Bush replies:
"Why, that is the precise reason I was gong to host a Poet's Symposium."

Socrates: "All right conduct depends on clear knowledge."

I like Laura Bush. I wish she were the president.
There is an uncomfortable silence
The president's lips remain still but the other parts of his face
seem to be going in ten different directions.

Socrates: "Knowledge is virtue.
 Contrariwise, ignorance is vice, and
no one can knowingly do wrong."

I love the way Socrates speaks.
"I agree with Socrates!
Knowledge is virtue.

And that goes for Iraq people as well.
That is why... well, you know Mrs. Bush
Over a decade ago when the president's father was president
And he started the Persian Gulf War
I couldn't sleep at night thinking of all those Iraqi conscripts
Our government was killing
I was told —two hundred in one blow
If I did sleep I'd wake up with my hair in knots..
From dreaming of what was going on
At the other side of the world beneath my pillow
So I said to my husband poet John Thomas..
Uh, Socrates, do you know John Thomas?

Socrates: "I know him well: large man; white beard;
Missing quit a few teeth; holds his sandals together
With paper clips..."

I say: "Yes. Well, that's from his belief in a life of dedicated poverty.
So I said to him: 'Let's bomb Iraq with poetry.'

And he said: "Oh yes. That will really bring Sadam to his knees."
But after awhile he realized what I said made sense and
We both began to write poems for the Iraqi people
and tie them to tiny parachutes; poems about a country
Founded on the freedom of speech
And an America so fine, that they would want to join us.
That was just my first suggestion for a non violent solution.
Because in the end, Mr. President, we're all just folks."
And thanks to the First Lady—
That's what poets are now doing across America.

The president pretends to be thinking out loud:
"Socrates is a doer of evil, and corrupter of the youth,
and he does not believe in the gods of the state."

I also pretend to be thinking out loud; shout:
"It appears to me, Mr. President, that
GREED IS YOUR DIETY!"
And politely say: "I think it's time to leave."

The president's lips are locked tight
But I know he's saying:
"EXECUTE THEM!"

It seems that Socrates could read those lips too
 Because outside the White House he murmurs:
"Execute us? If so –
he would injure himself more than
he would injure us. And I would rather die
having spoken after my manner
than speak in his manner and live."

"Ah Ha!" I exclaim:
"That sounds like something poet John Thomas would say!"
Then point to the flag above the White House
"Look ! It's a beautiful – just by itself
And even more for what it stands for.
It stands for freedom. Not an abstraction.
Freedom of speech – what we've just been exercising

Socrates does not look back.
He is accustomed to doing his thinking
In a Mediterranean climate
He walks, huddled in his light weight tunic
Against the Washington cold.
But I take one last look at how the White House
Looks after Socrates has visited
There seems a slight glow
And although there appears to be no wind
That flag is waving.

— February 12, 2003

ARISTOTLE AT A LAKER GAME
AND THE POETICS OF KOBE BRYANT

Aristotle has come as a guest of coach, Phil Jackson
So we sit in front row seats besides Jack Nicholson
"This is Los Angeles,"
I say to the ancient Greek philosopher
"Don't fret about your odd attire
The fans will think you're another actor
And it seems the team has read your Poetics
"And why am I hear?" He asks

I do not have to tell Aristotle
How to watch a Lakers basketball game
After all he wrote about "dramatic action"

He looks over the crowd at Staple Center
Says: "Poetry seems to have sprung
From deep within our nature
First, from the instinct for imitation..."

I leap from my seat:
"Imitation! Yes, Aristotle.
Look! There's Kobe Bryant!
I'm not certain what he imitates
But you are about to see a human being fly!"

The honorable philosopher remains seated
"I tell you: Kobe Bryant will fly
I know because... I...
Uh, I was the only one in my college class
Who got an 'A' in Logic!"

(Aye! Ye, gods and goddesses!
Why did I say that?
There is something about his demeanor
That makes one wish to impress
Aristotle is a snob)

Aristotle raises an eyebrow
I am embarrassed
I sit down, say softly:
"He will fly. I promise."

But he does not hear me
He is looking at Kobe
And first close look at him
Can do that kind of thing:
Stop one from listening
Directly before us
Kobe begins a 360 degree twist
This gives him lift
Still close to the floor
But now the propulsion begins

"Incidentally," I shout over the roar of the crowd:
"I like what you said, Aristotle, about poetry:
That the poets function is to describe,
Not the thing that has happened
But what might happen
Kobe will now attempt the might happen."

I whisper to myself:
"We humans are so cumbersome"
As Kobe's feet leave the floor
Begin to climb the sky

I like to watch this part
For the best effect
As if in slow motion
And in silhouette

On the way up
All the might happens are happening
Kobe clasps the ball like a raven's claw
Soars towards the hoop...

This is where with my minds eye I stop him
Mid air, hovering

It's happening so fast–
But, yes, nevertheless
Kobe is hovering

I could stay forever looking at him
At this point of stationary flight

And no matter how loud the crowd
Everything becomes quiet

Aristotle interjects from his Poetics:
"The Greek Chorus...
(which in this case means the fans)
Should be regarded as one of the actors."

"Yes. Shhhh."
(By this time I don't want to hear him talking)
" Shhhh. Yes. We're ALL hovering with Kobe."

It's mesmerizing: what Kobe does with the air
Or what the air does with him
A kind of welcoming
Why Kobe?
Perhaps its his concentration
Or heart. Yes.
I think it's Kobe Bryant's heart

The sky releases him
The ball falls through the hoop
(For me, an almost after thought)

On the ground Kobe smiles, licks his lips
He knows what he's just done
Although the fullness of it is comprehended
Only by some: Phil Jackson; obviously Jack Nicholson
And, of course, Aristotle
Who is now standing on his aristocratic toes

I no longer have to explain to him why he came
Not even the rules of the game
Nor that the Lakers are the World Champion Basketball Team

Lose or win: it's all the same
We came to see, and saw again
The gods becoming human beings

— February 22, 2003

INAUGURATION POEM FOR BILL ROSENDAHL

A hundred years ago, this very day, July 2, 1905, Venetians gathered to turn on 17, 000 light bulbs illuminating Venice of America. That light is now being passed to another century. We here today, are a result of those first Venetians' intentions as we gather to witness Bill Rosendahl take his oath of office as our Councilman. His intention: to both preserve and nurture that luminosity.

Raised in Venice, the very place in which he will take the oath, he is deeply connected to the land. "I try to live close to the earth," he says. And "My religion is simple: Love thy neighbor." Of him it is said: "He listens." And (this is true) a chicken will lay green eggs for him! There is both an unexplainable magic and a practical explanation for this. But the real question is— if he can nurture a chicken to the point where she will lay green eggs, what else can he do!?

Today, July 2, 2005, just before noon
In the full force of our Southern California sun
Before the Pacific Ocean
Surrounded by those whom he calls neighbor
As Bill Rosendahl speaks his oath of office
With him will be the voices of those
Who illuminated Venice 100 years ago
And with them our voices joining
In the full force of that original intention
To preserve and protect the body and soul of Venice

Venice, city conceived in imagination for imagination
With body intact –the canals, the welcoming houses
The people came. It happened – the magic — unexplainable
Venice becoming the city imagined
A city like no other city on earth
Its community of Venetians giving her a soul
Bright. Transcendent. The soul of Venice
A gift, which cannot be bought nor stolen
This is the gift out right, freely given
To those open to receive it; for those who listen

But Venice transcendent still needs a body
It can be, has been, wounded
It can die; live on only in history

So we here today, as with previous Venetians
Welcome all as neighbor, loving freely
At the same time preserve and protect our radiant city
With magic and practicality
And with the hope of a pale green egg
That resolve passed on from those that have gone before us
For them as for ourselves, and for those that will follow
Will stand here where we stand today
And who will walk upon our footsteps into the next century
That the light of Venice not be extinguished
Nor diminished, nor simply be maintained
But that light burn, burn, burn into a boundless luminosity!

POET LAUREATE ACCEPTANCE SPEECH

My first act as Poet Laureate is to define the word Epiphany.

It is: "To rent the veil." It is the reason we come to Venice.

It is what we get whether we want it or not – to live in the state of wonder.

And I humbly accept this position of being both the silence and voice of the wonder of Venice!"

Final Poems

POETRY IS THE DOOR TO INFINITY

The poem is
A shadow
Of lightning

An architecture of air
Muttering the mind of wind

BUG POEM FOR A THREE-YEAR-OLD

A bug is not a rug.
A bug is not a mug.
A bug is a bug!

If it sits upon your finger
You can lug a bug.
But sad, sad
You cannot hug a bug.

— May 11, 2003

SCRIPTURE OF THE MUSE

(John (and I) within — Memory Palace)

Tall shadow upon a
Lost balcony over invisible sea
I greet you.

The dark cannot be lost
Into the sudden night.
Golden thunder
To air to grasp
Blood is the light
No face

Strangers-
My veins
Invisible skies
As I leap
From the (last) balcony
Through the dark
Into the lost light.

THIS ROOM; THIS BURNING CITY

Does anything truly move at all
No (more) sermons to write.
No ruined abbeys to visit
Reduced to a single line.
And a wavering one.

No matter how many holes
I dig in the sand
The sea always wells up

This poem, this shipwreck
The time of the deed
Is part of the deed itself.

(And there are always the
black fountains).

I DREAM IN 2,200 DIFFERENT LANGUAGES

I dream in 2,200 languages
Wretched, hungry poems,
Written for no one

The lunatic laughter
No Divine madness
Behind closed windows
Puddles of moonlight
So far, no inspired lines
Lingering hopefully
In our dilapidated rooms
I cannot be buried
Uncertain invisible wanderers

Not yet.
But soon.

—May, 2003

FAR AWAY NOW

Far away now
The sacrament
The words themselves

The candle returns the flame

So few days
There are in certainty

Do shadows remember the sun?

Live slowly
Die slowly
It's our careful way of living.

Isolated from complexities
Of the ordinary world

Adapt to circumstances
No hurry
Become fragile

Out side it is
More

Here there is
Greater sympathy
Secrets are revealed

Alone in water
As one watching the sun

Envy nothing
In this solitude
Of wounds and kisses
Write as with fire
Ink of air.

The poem
A young mountain

Why us?
We have fallen.
Waiting to die
What have we done
To have fallen?

Waiting to die
Counting backwards

With tears
Shadows with tears
That cannot remember
The sun
In a sleep of blood
The flowers– blood
The rain– blood
On the windows
In a sleep of blood
That cannot be seen

I remember another sky
I have nothing to say
Until I return
From the living.

— May, 2003

WHISPERS BEFORE A TOMB
(OF MY HUSBAND, POET JOHN THOMAS)

It seems to me
Before our love
No pen could write
A poem that
Returned the word
To light

—June 13, 2003

*

Our love
Erodes time
Its memory
Has touch
Poems are its
Living ruins

—June 14, 2003

*

Do you dream, now, my Love?
And do I appear in them?

— July, 2003

*

Our love–
A species not yet evolved
And so blind it feels all.

— July, 2003

*

Although now silent
Your voice is stronger
Than any other's

— September 16, 2003

*

Love, Love
I would rather be in Hell with you
Than in Heaven with another

— September 21, 2003

THREE HAIKU

The wind is quiet
Outside your bedroom window
Yet my hair is tangled.

—June 28, 2003

*

That bright summer moon
It was a street lamp! But still–
A thousand kisses

—June 29, 2003

*

Your breath on my lips—
Only sound in the dark room
I– hardly breathing

—June 30, 2003

AMERICA

America
The light from your Statue of Liberty
Is being blown out
And your ears are so deafened by lies
You can barely hear yourself

America
You were young for two hundred years
So very young with
"The Blessings of Liberty to ourselves
And our Posterity" and "We, the People"
"Yearning to breathe free"
Beginning, always beginning
Your power, now being smothered
By the age-old will to power for a few

America
Your sense of truth and justice
Is being snuffed by those
Claiming truth and justice
Sending "The poor, the wretched" to prison
Often to "cruel and unusual punishment"
By ones who themselves should be jailed

America
You are dying
Lying on a floor in a jail cell
Gasping for air
Calling out for yourself

America
We *are* America
We are calling for ourselves
When things fall apart
Our center *does* hold

America
America hears you
We will begin again

IS THERE A RECIPROCITY?

Regarding our 100,000 couplings
Which you had said were real
Although the fingers were not

Is there a reciprocity
Of which I am unaware?

At night do ravens
Return their blackness to the sky?

By day do sunflowers
Burn the sun?

And most importantly
Is there a way
I may return you
To my touch?

—July 19, 2003

LITANY FOR PEGARTY

Pegarty, consider the possibility
in the trillion, billion, million
light years since the beginning of
this universe and I don't know precisely
how long afterwards it was with you
that I was once the same person
the very same person – only you
in this immensity of space
as well as time
I shared a womb
only with you
none other and I knew you
before you took your first breath
Pegarty, and you were the very first to
put your arm around me
in that same womb it was your arm
that consoled me
Pegarty, it was you who heard my first breath
and ever since we breathe together
for this, especially on our birthday
I am grateful, yes
in this expanding universe
of five billion years (is it?) none but you
Pegarty, with whom in this expanse
as well as others unknown to me
I floated timelessly in that womb where
we kicked and slept in the warmth
in the darkness from which I kicked you
out into the world at ten minutes to
ten o'clock on August 17, 1940
St. Vincent's Hospital I kicked you
out into the blazing light so that your cries
would be the first sounds in the trillion, billion
million to the trillionth, billionth, millionth power
of all sounds ever emitted, yes
so that yours would be
the first sound I would hear as
I emerged from the darkness and
now in my darkest hours it is always
your arm I feel
your voice that I hear

—August 17, 2003

ONE DIES HAPPILY

One dies happily
And with ease
When there's
No one left
To die.

— September, 2003

COLD ELLISON IX
(Unfinished Poem)

"Do you have the poems of Han-shan in your house?
They're better for you than any sutra reading!
Write them down and paste them on a screen
Where you can glance at them from time to time."
—Han-shan Cold Mountain

Now, when asked how I am
I reply: "Living without skin."
Each sinew exposed
It is as though I am a ghost
Peering through mesoderm

Flowers can get on my nerves
Since John...
(I cannot even now, seven months later say it)
I'll say shed his flesh ?? skin:
March 29, Good Friday at 3:00 p.m.

I read February entry in my journal
The month before...
"I dreamed to save him
I would have to give my skin
Become one of the 'skinless ones.'

In the dream before I signed I thought
"Better do this before I think about what I am doing"
As I signed the contract Jack Kerouac walked by—
He, too, was one of the skinless ones.

But the offering did not save John.
Odd – having forgotten about that dream
My answer always I am living without skin.

A knock
Lance Robbins (owner of the Ellison)
At the door
I tell him living without skin
He says that may be a good thing
Because of that sensitivity

Able to open – live. Feel his presence.
That it may always be like that
That art comes from pain.

I tell him how solitude is a solace
Here in our apartment in the Ellison
His eyes twinkle more than usual
He understands—he as John and I
So love this building.

It is a comfort knowing
To me it at times appears to be
A red brick Taj Mahal
At times: – a temple
Its sides could be a wailing wall
Or a California Gothic Cathedral
And (this even more now)
The apartment where great poems of the world...
Our apartment: a tabernacle.

He understands...
It is a comfort that he understands
And says:

Continue to speak to each other.
He says:
With energy or mental construction

But it is real —
I create John
Resurrect him.

The poems our sacrament

The Muse is hear (Did I write hear with an A?)
I mean here...
John and I lived... live
Both in flesh, now one spirit one half spirit / half flesh
Soon to be spirit.

Our poems
Our words

Flesh –
Into these bricks,

Wherever we go before

Whatever words or silences
Always here...

The Ellison

Tenants – never #31
Just called our apartment
"Where the poets live."

Lately I have come to think of our room as a tabernacle
So many of our poems written here
You on the bed
Lying on left side propped up by left elbow
Your writer's elbow
Pen over yellow pad
I a few feet away – in rocking chair you got for me
Looking at the sea – and beyond the sea
Just a few feet away
The space between us, I always felt
The length of the Muse.

Our poems – into this red brick
And – and – and –

The Ellison

I WISH TO DIE IN THE LAST THRUST OF

(Unfinished Poem)

"I wish to die pen in hand (know difficult to manage both.)"

Kilclousha. Philomene Long's mother (Maureen Coghlan) birthplace. Buttevant, Co. Cork, Ireland. Circa 1930s. Photographed by Maureen (Coghlan) Long

The Bristol House. 816 Russell St. Bristol, Virginia. Photographed by Nina Long

PLATE I

Philomene's father (Paul B. Long), football Hall of Fame. Emory and Henry College, Virginia. Circa 1920s. Photographed by Anonymous

Philomene's father, Naval Officer World War II. Circa 1940s. Photographed by Anonymous

PLATE II

Philomene's mother in her childhood.
Ireland. Circa 1910s.
Photographed by Anonymous

Philomene's mother in her twenties.
New York City. Circa 1930s.
Photographed by Anonymous

PLATE III

Philomene's sister (Pegarty), her mother (Maureen Long) and Philomene at the age of 2. Photographed by Paul B. Long

PLATE IV

*Philomene at first homesite –
17 Minetta Lane,
Greenwich Village, NYC.
Circa late 1990s.
Photographed by Pegarty Long*

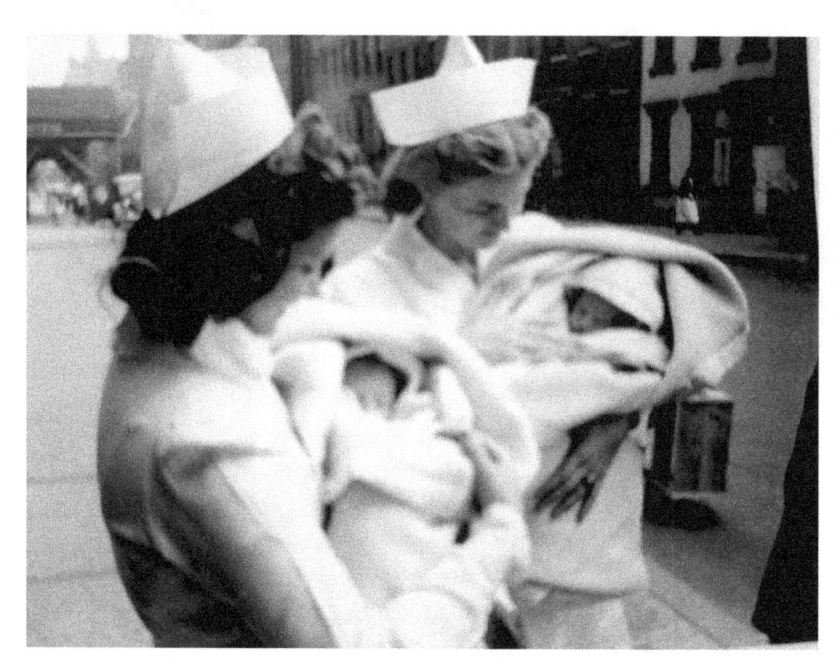

Philomene's birthplace. St. Vincent's Hospital. Greenwich Village, New York. Born August 17th, 1940. Leaving hospital with twin sister Pegarty. Photographed by Paul B. Long

PLATE V

Philomene at the age of 5, the year of her first poetic experience. 1945.
Photographed by Anonymous

PLATE VI

Pegarty and Philomene, Age 7. Philomene holding Danny the Duck for whom she wrote her first poem "Remember the Day" after his demise. Photographed by Maureen Long

First song. "Fatso Tree."

Philomene, Age 10. The year she wrote her first song (about her cat Fatso). Photographed by Maureen Long

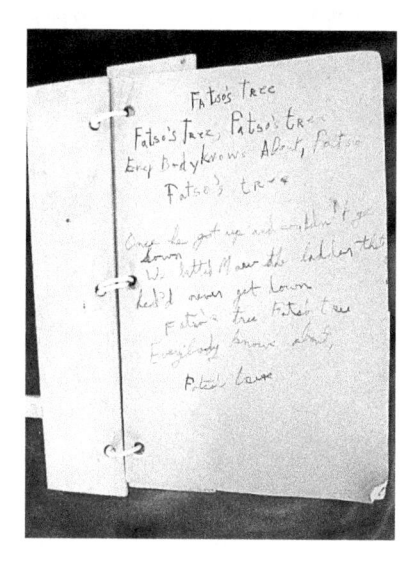

PLATE VII

First Holy Communion, Age 7. Philomene right of nun with sister. St. Anne's Catholic Church. Bristol, VA. Photographed by Anonymous

Philomene with her sister, Age 5. "Playing in the Southern Californian sun during World War II as the world fell apart." Coronado, San Diego, CA. Photographed by Maureen Long

PLATE VIII

Philomene, Age 12. Acting as The Blessed Virgin Mary. Pegarty as angel above her. Coco Solo, Panama. Photographed by Anonymous

Philomene, Age 10. Playing Annie Oakley. Photographed by Pegarty Long

Pegarty and Philomene, Age 7. First Holy Communion. Photographed by Paul B. Long

Pegarty and Philomene, Age 15. Jitterbugging in high school. The year that Philomene began to write poems earnestly. San Diego, California. Courtesy of The Academy of Our Lady of Peace

PLATE IX

Pegarty and Philomene, postulant. Sisters of St. Joseph of Carondelet. Age 18. The House of Studies and Mt. St. Mary's College, Los Angeles, California. Photographed by Dan Mitchell

Friend (Dick Wolsfelt) sister, Philomene and aunt (Ellen Mitchell) same day. Photographed by Dan Mitchell

Letter to father from Sr. Marie Philomene (Nov. 1960, fourth line, top paragraph) in which she writes - "I am drawn to writing poetry."

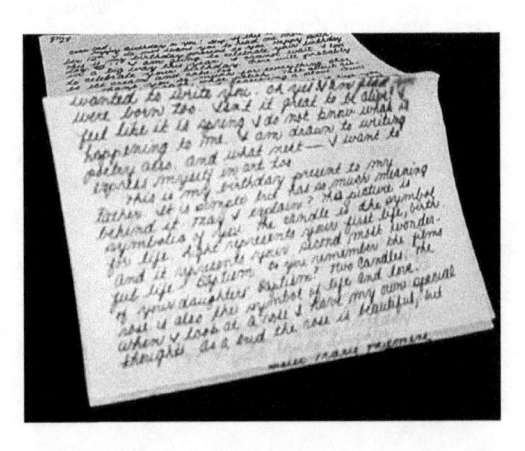

PLATE X

Sister Marie Philomene. 1961. Photographed by Dan Mitchell

PLATE XI

*Pegarty with guitar.
New York City. 1965
"Pegarty, with whom I floated
timelessly in that womb where
we kicked and slept in the warmth
in the darkness... and now in my
darkest hours it is always your
arm I feel your voice that I hear"
Photographed by Philomene Long*

"On the Road With Pegarty" Pegarty and Philomene on the road and Europe "as I ran away – ran ran to the Queen Mary – sailed the Atlantic..." 1963. Photographed by Nina Long

PLATE XII

*Philomene as the Muse. "The Visitation of the Muse" series. Early 1980s.
Photographed by Pegarty Long*

Painter Roger Penney in his studio. Above him are paintings included in collaboration with the poetry of Philomene in their book from his series which Philomene based her book of poetry, "Odd Phenomenon in an Abandoned City". "Roger Penney-Death cannot close your eyes." San Diego, California. Early 1980s. Photographed by Philomene Long

PLATE XIII

THE BEATS AT THE FOX

A VHS Copy of "The Beats."

Philomene with her Bolex 16mm movie camera. One of the cameras she used while shooting "The Beats An Existential Comedy." 1980s. Photographed by Pegarty Long

Jason Kugelman and Philomene on the air at KPFK Radio Los Angeles. Late 1970s. Photographed by Pegarty Long

PLATE XIV

Philomene with Beat Poet Stuart Perkoff. Venice, CA. Early 1970s. Photographed by Shirley Fiske

Philomene in her "The Beats An Existential Comedy" t-shirt. Early 1980s. Photographed by Pegarty Long

PLATE XV

Philomene with Beat Poet Allen Ginsberg. Early 1980s. Photographed by Jason Kugelman

Philomene with author Timothy Leary. Venice, CA. Mid 1990s. Photographed by Anonymous

PLATE XVI

Cover photo for their collaborated book of love poems to each other, "The Book of Sleep".
Beat Poet John Thomas "my only one" and Philomene Long. Venice, CA.
Photographed by Pegarty Long

PLATE XVII

John Thomas and Philomene with Beat Poets: David Meltzer, Frank Rios, Tony Scibella and Aya in front at a celebration of the publication of Venice Beat Poet, Stuart Perkoff's Collected Poems. Beyond Baroque Literary Center. Venice, CA 1990s. Photographed by Pegarty Long

*Poets Scott Wannberg, Philomene, S. A. Griffin, John Dorsey and Philomene celebrate with a Royal Poet's Breakfast at Philomene's home in The Ellison. Early 2000s.
Photographed by Lorraine Perrotta*

Novelist Mariana Dietl and Philomene in The Ellison. Venice, CA Photographed by Mara Marenco

PLATE XVIII

"Beat No Chaser" poster

Philomene reading at "Beat No Chaser" poetry event.
Hollywood, CA. Early 1990s. Photographed by Pegarty Long

John Thomas and Philomene signing books at publication of "Bukowski in the Bathtub" publication reading and celebration. Beyond Baroque. Venice, CA. 1997. Photographed by Pegarty Long

PLATE XIX

Fred Dewey, Director of Beyond Baroque, speaking at the David Amram musical event. Early 2000s. Photographed by Pegarty Long

Herbert B. Fishberg at Beyond Baroque. Early 2000s. Photographed by Margaret Molloy

Poet Holly Prado and Actor-Poet Harry Northup at the Playboy Mansion, Brentwood, CA. Early 2000s. Photographed by Raymond Benson.

John and Philomene together at the doors of Beyond Baroque after the Bukowski in the Bathtub publication celebration. Venice, CA. Late 1990s. Photographed by Pegarty Long

Poet Mariano Zaro gives Philomene a good laugh after her featured poet reading at LACMA, The Los Angeles County Museum of Art. Late 1990s. Los Angeles, CA.

Philomene reads birthday poem to author V. Virom Coppola after a good Italian meal. Los Angeles, CA. Early 2000s. Photographed by Herbert B. Fishberg

Filmmaker Peter McCarthy and Philomene at "Bukowski in the Bathtub" publication celebration. Venice, CA. Late 1990s. Photographed by Pegarty Long

Poet Michael C Ford, John Thomas and Philomene. Santa Monica, CA. Mid 1990s. Photographed by Pegarty Long

PLATE XX

Maureen Luna Long and Patrick Moore, Philomene' children, on Mother's Day at the Fig Tree., Venice Boardwalk. Venice, CA. Early 1990s. Photographed by Philomene Long

Philomene with granddaughter Tara, "Buddha Princess." Mid 2000s. Photographed by Pegarty Long

Adam Sandman. The son-in-law and father. Maryland. Mid 2000s. Photographed by Maureen Luna Long

Philomene with grandson Aidan, "Little fire." Venice, CA. Mid 2000s. Photographed by Maureen Luna Long

Philomene and Maureen on her high school graduation day. Late 1970s. Photographed by Anonymous

PLATE XXI

Philomene and John Thomas' last reading together, dressed in wedding attire to read for Gregory Corso's "Marriage". Beyond Baroque. Early 2000s. Photographed by Pegarty Long

Philomene, poets Tony Scibella and poet Jack Micheline after "Beat No Chaser" reading. Hollywood, CA. Early 1990s. Photographed by Pegarty Long

Poet Wanda Coleman and Pegarty Long. Early 2000s. Photographed by Margaret Molloy

John Thomas with Venice's Poet Laureate Philomene Long and San Francisco's Poet Laureate, Jack Hirschman. Early 2000s. Photographed by Anonymous

PLATE XXII

Philomene and John on the Venice Boardwalk bench at Ocean Front Walk and Paloma Ave. near The Ellison. "They are already ghosts John and Philomene as they pass along the Boardwalk this highway of poetry and death where ghosts and poets overlap." Venice, CA. Mid 1990s. Photographed by Pegarty Long

Philomene at John Thomas' interment. Holy Cross Cemetery. Inscription on gravestone . "Our life The One Secret That Surprises Death." Culver City, CA. 2002. Photographed by Pegarty Long

PLATE XXIII

Philomene, the ordained Queen of Bohemia at her writing desk in The Ellison. Venice, CA. Mid 1990s. Photographed by Pegarty Long – Below is a selection of covers from published works.

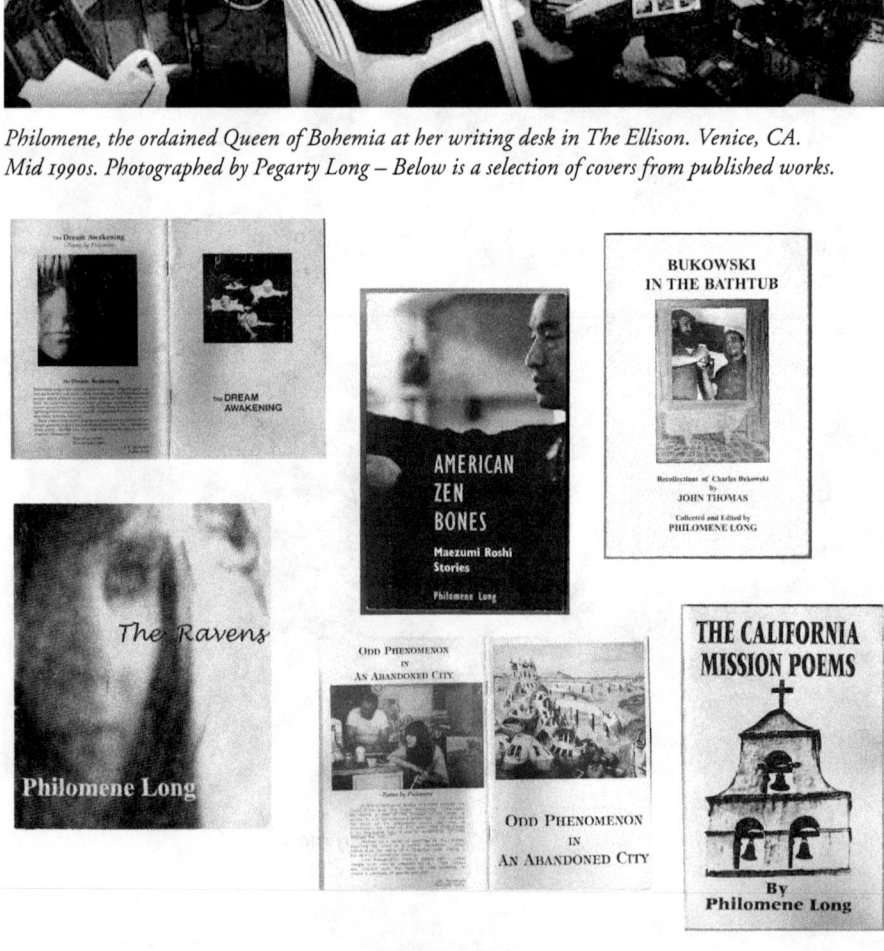

PLATE XXIV

"Venice, Holy ground, stained with the blood of poets." Lines from a poem of Philomene's engraved on "The Poetry Wall" near the Venice Boardwalk and Windward. Early 2000s. Photographed by Jeff Leahy

Philomene after reading her inauguraion poem for Councilman Bill Rosendahl's inauguration. Mayor Riordan, Councilman Bill Rosendahl, Mayor Villaraigosa, and Philomene. July 4th, 2005. Photographed by Pegarty Long

Philomene Long becomes the Poet Laureate of Venice. Sept. 24th, 2002. "My first act as Poet Laureate is to define the word Epiphany. It is: 'To rent the veil.' It is the reason we come to Venice. It is what we get whether we want it or not – to live in the state of wonder!"

Venetians celebrate the lighting of the new Venice sign at Danny's Deli on Windward. Nancy McCulloch, Jim Smith, an editor of Venice's newspaper **"The Free Venice Beachhead"** and Philomene. June, 2007. Photographed by Jeff Leahy

PLATE XXV

Pegarty and Philomene on the set of "The Irish Vampire Goes West", starring Philomene. Los Angeles. Early 2000s. Photographed by Brogan De Paor

Philomene in Pegarty Long's photographic series "The Visitation of the Muse. The Muse Comes." Early 1980s. Photographed by Pegarty Long

PLATE XXVI

*Pegarty and Philomene's last birthday together, four days before Philomene died. August 17th, 2007.
Photographed by Herbert B. Fishberg*

*Philomene as the muse from the photographic series, "The Visitation of the Muse. The Muse Leaves."
Early 1980s. Philomene dies August 21st, 2007 on her mother's birthday.
Photographed by Pegarty Long*

PLATE XXVII

The Crypt. Holy Cross Cemetery, 2007. Photographed by Pegarty Long

PLATE XXVIII

Index of First Lines

10,000 years. 500 tribes and tribelets, *143*

A bug is not a rug, *307*

A door opened then closed forever, *146*

A faint suggestion of a smile, *6*

A full moon, *75*

A good day for a Bukowski funeral, *198*

A hundred years ago, this very day, July 2, 1905, Venetians gathered, *301*

A memory shaped from adobe, *139*

A reddish brown sky in her hair, *203*

A swan in the cemetery's pond, *287*

After death of Baby Cahiermie, *25*

After five years cloistered in a Catholic convent above Los Angeles, *21*

All dream - and whose? *260*

All lies in utter darkness now, *11*

All thought is memory, *62*

Allen Ginsberg burning shadow of Blakean angel, *214*

Although now silent, *314*

America, *316*

Among grass and trees she walked, *18*

An orange is, *25*

Aristotle has come as a guest of coach, Phil Jackson, *298*

As a young boy my son Patrick saved the lives of neighborhood insects, *252*

At cemetery widowers, mostly, *276*

Atrial Fibrillation, *167*

Before the stars were, *90*

Behind broken gates, *137*

Between the death and the weeping, *183*

Beyond your circle, *80*

Black clock of carefully placed tears, *157*

Born of Fire and blood, *140*

Burning blue bell of time before the great unmade bed, *263*

Cold cliffs more beautiful, *118*

Cold eye burning, *74*

Come, my love, *97*

Cracked glass mirrors cast rainbows, *220*

Crushed pigeon on the pavement, *227*

Do you dream, now, my love?, *314*

Dodger Stadium, 1988 World Series Los Angeles Dodgers & Oakland Athletics, *281*

Does anything truly move at all, *309*

Dry, dry and sharp, *170*

Each morning I detach them, *256*

Erin the land itself a phantom, *159*

Even if it lies, *171*

Every poem I write is a suicide, *106*

Faint tremors, *108*

Far away now, *311*

I

Index of First Lines

Gentle Lightning, 247
Green the hours, 138

He lay with his eyes closed, 13
He said he liked fine women, 35
He was choking me and
  pulling my face off, 172
Heaven kissed her, 17
Her name is Sally Benedict, 2
Her own tears awaken her, 108
Here I stand, 4
Hers was the first cry that I heard
  in my first morning, 209
His eyes show me things so small, 226
How close to birth, 108
How few days there are, 108

I am no longer afraid of this poem, 104
I am not here, 136
I am not of this world, 267
I am the poem, 63
I awaken every morning with
  the rhythms of the train, 210
I awaken to go to sleep, 109
I dream in 2,200 languages, 310
I had a mother, 28
I had dropped a can of Pepsi
  in a Venice alley, 206
I have fondness for them, 266
I have the Irish taste, 173

I heard a voice saying, 151
I must speak softly the flowers, 164
I never thought it would be like this, 39
I pray with an ungodly haste, 54
I remember I thought I was a cat, 87
I step inside the poem, 232
I used to be fairly poor, as poor goes, 123
I walk out on the beach
  only one pink cloud, 254
I walked to the seashore, 7
I watch from inside a portrait, 223
I wish the wind would not blow, 36
I wish to die pen in hand
  (know difficult to manage both.), 323
I'll show you something subtle, 84
It's Midnight Mass, the church is still, 16
I've seen too much of what, 38
Idle floating continents, 88
Imagine your father is Goliath, 292
In every raven's beak, 241
In the forests of Central America, 182
In the privacy of mirrors, 261
In the shining Black wound of night, 202
Inside the California Mission
  of Santa Barbara, 288
Inside this bleeding lyric, 289
Ireland whose warriors fought
  their battles naked, 156
It has its own mind, the past, 145
It is difficult to know, 77

Index of First Lines

It is half-past-four in the afternoon
 your fall the sound of, 221
It is his vision, 46
It is not the end, 42
It seems to me before our love, 313
It was as though the stars themselves, 48
It was not a gentle passing, 52
It's not easy to share a womb, 43

"Jack" I said, "Walt Whitman had
 nightmares of you", 215
John Thomas critical mass, 95
John Thomas, stretched upon the bed, 99
John Thomas: stretched upon a gurney, 275

Last night I wandered to the sea, 12
Last night John Thomas dreamed
 of a pen that writes in gold, 208
"Little fire" sets off all our fire detectors, 259
Living in the mountains, mind ill at ease, 125
Long ago, when I was young, 10
Lord, I asked you, 37
Los Angeles: City over cracked stone, 265
Love, Love, 314
Love, you are green and dark, 89

Madam, Sir whichever you prefer, 280
Maltreatment of a house fly, 265
Maureen—Over the quiet ice, 205
May I congratulate you, 96

May we see with their eyes, 153
Memory is debris, 265
Mind my bullet wound, 180
Mirrors are sleeping winds, 233
Moments pass by in emptiness, 5
My first act as Poet Laureate is to define
 the word "Epiphany," 303
My heart is heavy with unshed tears, 8
My life has been a terrified eye, 235
My little Buckaroo, 174
My skull is full with conversations of stars, 64

Night climbs the purple grasses, 229
Now death is in collision, 249
Now have the eyes of a ghost, 76
Now she is where there, 108
Now we need (In Okefenonkee anyway), 165
Now, when asked how I am, 320

Old fool!, 166
On your behalf, Valarie and Kent, we have
 invoked Mnemosyne, Memory, 255
One can never see a raven without hearing
 a poem, 240
One dies happily, 319
Our flesh, now a dazzling sepulcher, 250
Our life this poem, 286
Our love erodes time, 313
Our love, 314
Over the threshold of joy, 44

Index of First Lines

Palaces and colonnades, cities, 185
Passion does not go without a curse: 217
Patients in canary yellow hospital gowns, 102
Pegarty, consider the possibility, 318
Poems are living ruins, 265
Poems are the world asleep, 224
Poet's job, 26
Poetry, 20
President George Bush and First Lady Laura Bush, 294
Proud, sullen world, 246
Push anything to its extreme, 108

Reason is cruel, 103
Refuse to sleep, 50
Regarding our 100,000 couplings, 317
Rooms, rooms without walls, 81
Scribe: Beati mortui, 150
Shadows are a slow hysteria, 265
Shall I compare you to a winter's night?, 204
She adjusts a chair for a ghost", 279
She is full of sleep, 109
She is the mountains, 51
She's a Ms. Prufrock held together with unease, 277
Shirley, your camera like a needle in broken rooms, 219
Silence drifts down, 148
Silver days at the Ellison, 129
Soledad. Solitude, 142

Sometimes I feel I can hear her, 116
Stone of melancholy, 85
Summer '85, 91

Tall shadow upon a lost balcony over invisible sea I greet you, 308
That bright summer moon, 315
The Blessed Padre who once walked under, 135
The carcasses of imagery, 265
The cats always the cats, 83
The City of Angels has its hermits, 207
The darkness which covers the earth, 149
The devil possesses more faith, 108
The earth is not a refuge, 175
The earth, too, is afraid I tell you, 195
The Hermit sits in the center of the stage, 107
The marble corpus dangles, 274
The moon if it could would be a Raven, 243
The mountains are passionate and still, 66
The mountains are passionate and still, 67
The mountains come bouncing and roaring into the room, 197
The olive tree, 141
The Padres cut crosses, 134
The poem comes its currents brush my lips, 176
The poem is a shadow of lightning, 306
The poem is composed largely of the hunger, 230
The poem takes a hundred years to come, 105

Index of First Lines

The poem transfers its force to the reader, 278

The poet lay like a fallen tree, 49

The purple curtain moves, 82

The scream, 100

The sea – a forever startling, 264

The still point from when and where we began, 265

The velvet claw, 25

The whistling winds, 161

The white mist came over the sea, 55

The wind is quiet, 315

The wind pushed us, 45

The world, is it called the "rolling void"?, 257

There are bad dreams, 108

There are no answers, 40

There s no comfort in the poem, 177

There, the wheels to rail a softer sound a softer pitch, 262

These nightly vigils, 79

These poems do not know, 62

They are already ghosts John and Philomene, 237

This crime of Heaven, 248

This is a dynamic account of blinking and breathing, 131

This is the Garden, Adam, and you've just eaten the Apple, 258

This is the morning, 92

Through your forehead, 62

Time is not an abstraction, 265

To slice the voice open, 234

Today Venice is a mysterious, a lonely, a solitary, 191

Tonight's thin fog, 168

Twenty years I have sat by this river, 71

Two and a half years (on and off), 121

Under the skin of life: 225

Venice Holy Ground (original), 69

Venice Holy Ground, 68

Warm summery days, 127

We await, 41

We don't know, 108

We open a door to where there is no road, 231

We waited only for Remembrance, 53

We will lie, 47

Wedged between, 285

What was that sound?, 70

When daylight fades, 15

When I awoke I was saying, 78

When life on earth, 14

Where can I hide my love for you? 88

Which way to turn, 9

While passing through Bristol, 3

Winter, 2002, I walk out to the sunset sea, 270

With my hands in the snow, 169

Index of First Lines

With you I am a nun again, 88

Within this darkness the light, 152

You are sleeping, my love, 98

You are worldly, Sister Marie Philomene," 195

You don't do much, 33

You have filled me with your seas, 34

You sit, my love, a crumpled man in a hospital wheel chair:, 271

You think you exist, 109

You're packing to go, 29

Your breath on my lips, 315

Your Holiness, Pope John Paul II, 110

Your kiss (was it a kiss?), 86

ABOUT THE AUTHOR

Philomene Long was the daughter of a naval officer and a mother Who emigrated from Ireland to America to become a writer. She grew up in New York City; Bristol, Virginia and San Diego. She went to Catholic schools, and graduated from The Academy of Our Lady of Peace and Mount St. Mary's College. She also earned a Master of Arts degree at UCLA. Her vocation as a nun came at age seven, and she entered the convent *"as a rather wild teenager."* She became, as John Maynard says, *"a rather wild nun."* A friend in the convent told Long about Venice and told her as well that she was a *"beatnik."* When Long asked why, her friend replied, *"Because you spend so many hours looking at the sky."* After a failed marriage, Maynard goes on, *"she moved to Venice to write poetry, shoot film, and live exactly as she chose."* She became *"a regular feature of the Ocean Front in her tennis shoes, black thrift-shop dresses, long, straight hair, alarm-clock pendant, and heavy silver cross."* She met Venice Beat Poet Perkoff in 1973. After his death she continued to live in Venice—and, thirty four years later, she was *"still around in force."*

Over the years Long published many books of poetry, including two collaborations with her husband of 18 years, poet John Thomas: The Book of Sleep and The Ghosts of Venice West. She lived a life of poetry and *"dedicated poverty"* with him until his death in 2002. She also made films, including *The Beats: An Existential Comedy*, with Allen Ginsberg, and *The California Missions*, with Martin Sheen. She was named *"The Queen of Bohemia"* by her poetry peers. She became the Poet-Laureate of Venice in 2005.

She died suddenly after a brief illness in her beloved home The Ellison in Venice, California on August 21st, 2007, the day of her mother's birthday and four days after her own 67th birthday. She was found dressed in white, the color that she preferred to dress in when she wrote, lying next to her writing table with arm and hand outstretched towards —

Night King

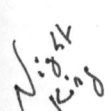